Potty Training for REAL Cats

Cat Toilet Training for Humans & Felines

Cassie Cluster

Published by Picky Press.

Potty Training for REAL Cats

Cat Toilet Training for Humans and Felines

Copyright © 2021 Cassie Cluster

OdorMute™ picture used with permission from HT-Pet, LLC

Cover Design, all other photographs and pictures are copyright Cassie Cluster.
Front Cover: "Katerina All Grown Up",
Back Cover/Title Page: "Baby Katerina in Potty Training".

Print ISBN: 9781643949963

EBook ISBN: 9781643949970

Library of Congress Control Number: 2021931954

Author Contact: Cassie.Cluster63@gmail.com

Published by Picky Press, an imprint of Tovim Press, LLC.
Phoenix, Arizona, USA.

PickyPress.com

Potty Training for REAL Cats

Cat Toilet Training for Humans & Felines

Cassie Cluster

Dedicated to Mum with Love

This book would not be complete without mentioning my whole-hearted gratitude to my mother, to whom this work is dedicated to. Having been raised on a farm, she instilled in me a love of creatures of all kinds, *especially* cats. (She earned the family nickname "Grandma Cats".) We shared our home with nearly every type of critter from rats to cats, dogs to pollywogs.

All my life, she has patiently put up with me bringing home every stray kitten or cat, having up to ten at one time (only three of which were from the ten examples in this book). She spared no expense to take care of them from food to vet bills, usually without complaint.

I will always remember the happy times in life that we shared with our rather large feline family. I hope you enjoy the collages that I put together of some of the special cats that we (or I) have shared our lives with, and travelling down memory lane as to many of the cats and how they came to be with us.

Thank You Mum, for all you have done!

Table of Contents

(Chapter 4 Continued)

Chapter 5 ~ Tips for Smooth Training and Transition

Chapter 6 ~ Basic Training ~ Get with the Program!

Chapter 7 ~ When Problems Arise

Snip, my very first cat in 1971, a 12-week-old purebred Persian.

Introduction

The title of this book was partially inspired by a comment someone made when they saw a picture of two of my cats using the toilet: "Is this for real?" The premise is self-explanatory, being based on real cats and actual experiences of over 30 years. Although many people make light of the subject, it is really a serious business. Much of cat toilet training has to do with the kitty, its personality and physical traits. However, it also has just as much to do with the human "trainer", and the interaction with their cat.

Certain myths are dispelled, such as "every single cat is able to be completely trained", a cat will only take X amount of time to potty train, and the litter box itself must be at the same height as the toilet before they start to learn.

I hope to cover every possible situation that may come up, and go over the different aspects that help to determine if your cat is a good candidate (or not). Fortunately, most cats *are* good candidates, but this book can help deal with some of the little "quirks" that can come up. You will get to "meet" ten of my cats that were potty-trained, hear their various stories, and see what makes each cat "tick". I have pictures of many of the cats, although at times there was no camera available to document the "potty process" for everyone. And just to note, I never taught them to flush. Since cats are so clean in general, they would be flushing all day!

Cat Potty Training: The Ideal vs. Reality

The Ideal: You come home to a spotless house, your friends come in and remark how there is no "cat smell" (nicely inferring that there is no litter box aroma), and your bathroom is always spotless, clean and tidy. While all of these things can be a reality, (at least eventually), it takes some hard work on the part of all participants!

Cat Potty Training sounds like great fun, a wonderful conversation piece for parties or talk around the office. If you want to train your cat for notoriety, just for the novelty, strictly to save money on litter, or to avoid cleaning the litter box, don't buy this book! It is meant for the serious person who loves their cat(s) and wants them to be happy, healthy, and above all, as stress-free as possible.

Rule number one for cat potty training is, the cat needs to be comfortable and relaxed! Most humans are like that too, as they read a magazine, or skim articles on their phone as they are in the bathroom to relax. Your cat is no different! So, when in doubt, always put yourself in the cat's place. If there are any anxious moments, you will need to keep calm as well, *for the cat's sake.*

🐾 🐾 🐾 🐾

The Reality: It isn't for *every* cat. Part of this is due to the lack of patience, or knowledge of how to act or treat the cat on

2

the human's part. During the training period, it isn't always going to be pretty. There will possibly be accidents, and for at least a month or two, your bathroom will not be spotless and tidy, but may look more like a tornado hit it!

"Potty Training for REAL Cats" is based on over 30 years of experience training various cats with vastly different personalities. The reality is, not every single cat is fit for "using the potty". If you keep your expectations low, you will be much happier, and may be pleasantly surprised in the end. This said, my success rate in training cats to use the human toilet was 100%. The truth however, is that only about 70% succeeded in *remaining* completely potty-trained without "accidents" (or should I say, "accidentally on purpose").

The 30% of cases could be ruled out almost immediately by knowing the cat's traits. A mere 10% was due to a physiological problem, and was no fault of the cat whatsoever. Another 10% were "difficult" cats, which most people probably do not have in their homes anyway, and the last 10% just simply didn't like going on the toilet and made it very much known.

Before you start actual training, it is essential to read this book. Cat toilet training takes immense patience, diligence, and above all, consistency. Depending on the cat, it may or may not be a very long process. In all cases, the training process has much to do with the personality of the cat and how close the "Pet Parent" is with the cat. A cat should preferably be at least 4-5 months old, otherwise, they are too small to fit on the potty, and not mature enough to make rational decisions. (Yes, cats are big on decision making, mostly on whether any given situation is good for them or not.) This is when being a properly trained "Pet Parent" comes into play.

If you are prepared to spend the first few days staying at home with the cat, you will be rewarded with a "cat's lifetime" of benefit. Do know that once a cat is potty-trained, it can never be an indoor/outdoor cat because it would ruin the potty training. This is a good thing, because indoor cats can be happy living in small quarters, and are safe from dangers like cars, diseases, and predators.

All in all, the time you spend training is well worth the end result, and will bring you and your kitty closer.

Chapter 1

What Is Needed Before You Start

Cleaning and Preparations

Clean It Well! Before you even start training, make sure the bathroom is ready. If it isn't already, clean the bathroom thoroughly, paying special attention to the toilet, and the floor around and areas in back of the toilet. Cats are extremely sensitive to smells, and old urine smell can throw them off. Be sure to rinse well, so there is no potentially toxic residue that the cat can get into and wash off of themselves.

If you don't know the history of your living space, like a new apartment, etc., and it looks clean but you would really like to be sure, there is an excellent way to find out just how clean it is. Get a small "UV-A" black light flashlight, or a black light bulb in a lamp. Turn out the lights and shine the black light onto the surfaces around the toilet in the bathroom. Urine will glow in the black light, and then you know exactly where to clean and disinfect. If it is visible enough for you see it in the blacklight, odds are the cat can smell it. This is an excellent tool to have around in case you ever suspect there has been an accident.

Temporary Barriers: These items (such as inverted small trash cans or large drink bottles filled with water are used to take up space on a flat surface. In pretty much all of my experiences, (and others that I have read about), the cats like to go around the back of the toilet or around the sides near the back. Discourage this behavior before it even happens! They like flat areas, where they feel comfortable and safe to go.

Place barriers around the toilet, only allowing the cat to

get up on the toilet from the front and slightly to the sides. Save large drink jugs to fill and place them all around. These work the best to make excellent barrier since they have weight to them. If you have a large gravity waterer or fountain, this helps take up room too. A small scratching post will work. These send the psychological message that this is not the place to relieve oneself. Barriers will only be temporary, until your cat is completely trained. After using the potty has become a habit (Graduation Day), it should be safe to take the barriers away after a couple of weeks. It has to be ingrained in their brain that they are supposed to use the toilet.

Occasionally, cats may choose to go in a bathroom

sink. It is fairly logical. Many rounder sinks have a similar shape to a toilet, and cats tend to smell the drain and relate it to it. It is something they can sit in to go like a litterbox, and don't have to mess with perching on a ledge. If a cat chooses to go there, simply put something over the sink to cover it, or put something like an easily removable bottle in it. It should be anything to discourage them and make going there "uncomfortable".

If you have a bathtub or shower in the same room, the next most likely place cats will choose to eliminate is the tub. (Flat and safe!) It is a major plus if you already have a simple glass shower door that closes off the area. If this is not possible, fill the tub with easily-removable, large bulky items, more water jugs, items on top of boxes, etc. For a while, it may look like a tornado hit your bathroom, but the objective is to make this an "unsafe" non-flat area that is totally unattractive to them. Another idea is fill it with water, if the drain plug works. (It can get dirty and start to grow algae over time, so it isn't great.)

🐾 🐾 🐾 🐾

Essentials

A "To Die For" Potty Treat: The treat given has to be so irresistible that the cat will do just about anything to get it. This is the main drive for the cat once it connects the treat with going in the toilet.

7

🐾 The "Potty Treat" can be any special treat, either made for giving occasional, or even a favorite food.

🐾 For very picky cats, it could be some tuna juice or a bit of cooked chicken.

🐾 For those rare cats that don't care about food at all, they may like having interactive play time, or an extra-long petting session. (On a side note, I don't recommend laser pointers. They are great fun for the human to watch, but the ultimate in frustration for a feline, trying desperately to catch something it never can, and getting exhausted or dizzy in the process.)

The treat will be given every single time the cat successfully goes on the toilet. It can be started right away, or can be given at PHASE 2. At first, they may not connect the treat with the potty, but after a while, the proverbial "light bulb goes on" in the cat's brain and it starts to make sense to them that the two are directly connected. Of course, a whole lot of praise and attention goes along with it.

In my home, a Potty Treat is commensurate with the amount of difficulty, so I usually give one piece of treat for "#1", and two pieces of treat for "#2". This is not a hard and fast rule, but the cats seem to appreciate the fact that I know the latter is much more difficult for them.

The Toilet Trainer: It is essential to have some sort of potty trainer kit. It can ideally be bought, or you can even make your own. The trainer I first used 30 years ago is no longer available, but there seem to be several good designs out there. I would check on reviews of the various trainers first before purchasing one.

A homemade trainer pan can be made out of a variety of materials, but the main idea is the same. (See D.Y.I.s in Appendix on page 171.) First it must hold the weight of litter and a cat. Then gradually it has an ever-widening hole in the center, until the bottom is non-existent.

Once the cat is trained, I highly recommend to keep the old trainer set. Clean it up and store it away in a box where the cat cannot see it. Though it might be tempting to toss it once you are reveling in the success of a properly toilet trained kitty, it can actually come in very handy later if there is ever a time of unforeseen circumstances, such as illness (either of a human or cat), relocation, and additional cats coming into the family. It is great for re-training a cat who had a hiatus, or first-time training. Now you have the experience with it already for training.

The "Temporary" Litter: You won't be needing it once the cat is trained, but it does need to have certain qualities.

🐾 *Never* use clumping litter, as this interferes with some trainers, causing them to clog if they have holes, and is certainly not good for plumbing. It usually contains silica, which is not even good for the cat! If you have leftover clumping litter, and it's all you have for PHASE 1 while it is still being used as a litterbox and being cleaned out as normal, that's okay. However, it *must* be changed for PHASE 2.

🐾 Use plain old clay litter. It is tried and true, and much healthier for the cats. Even better, use flushable litter made for the purpose.

🐾 Try to avoid litters with perfumes. A cat needs some "kitty scent" in order to get stimulated to go, and connect that it is a potty. A cat's nose is far more sensitive than ours. They can have perfume allergies. I'm allergic to perfume. It can give me migraines, and my sense of smell isn't nearly as keen as a cat's.

A tiny bit of litter in the potty is not going to wreck your plumbing (unless it's the clumping type). Toilets are designed to take large solids. This doesn't mean you should intentionally dump a lot in, but if your toilet can't take a few granules of clay litter, there is something wrong with your plumbing!

A Proper Toilet Seat: This is perhaps the single most important piece of "equipment" you can have. The ideal toilet seat would be lidless, but these can be hard to find except for "commercial" designs.

🐾 A nice flat seat (below, top) is a plus, even if it is in wood. Keep it clean and it shouldn't be a problem.

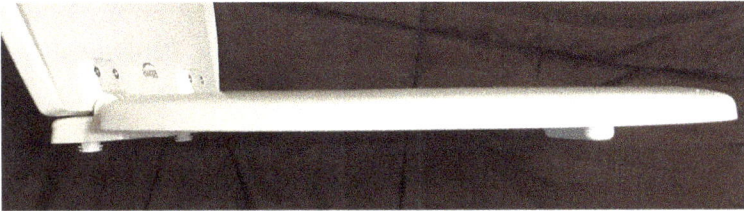

🐾 The plain old cheaper flat wood seats (top) are getting harder to find, in favor of easy-to-clean molded plastics (above bottom). Plastic is great for easy cleaning, but there has been a recent phenomenon of the seats being molded and shaped for human comfort. They may be designed to fit the human posterior, but are not very cat-friendly. These are very slippery and curvy, actually pitching the cat toward the water. It doesn't make it very easy for the cat to balance on while they are doing their business, especially if they have a lot of fur on their feet between their paw pads. (The "Furry-Footed").

🐾 Ignore "slow-close" toilet seats, that is a disaster waiting to happen! You will not need it.

🐾 Lidless seats are ideal, as guests would not accidentally put the lid down, and the lid *must be kept up at all times*.

🐾 Ideally, get a seat with simple hinges affixed with screws, and remove the lid completely.

🐾 A soft vinyl seat might be good if it is more of a matte finish. If you do not trim your cat's claws, they could potentially rip it. Having claws even if just trimmed, does help the cat to feel safe and like they are hanging on to something.

🐾 🐾 🐾 🐾

Additional Assets

🐾 ***Shower Door:*** If you don't have one, it's a great idea to invest in a shower door. One of the main complaints I have heard is that cats choose to go in the bathtub or shower. There is a certain logic to it. The cats smell the wastewater in the drain, which it smells somewhat like toilet water. Most of the time, they will actually go on toilet water. Most of the time, they will actually go on the drain itself, rather than choose other parts of the tub. (Pretty smart!)

Some Pet Parents would rather just compromise and allow the cat to do their business in the tub, and clean it up as needed. This is may seem like a good compromise, but it is far from ideal. If the cat repeatedly urinates on the drain it can be very corrosive and eat into the finish of the drain cover, or possibly even cause an enameled steel tub to start to rust underneath the drain cover, unseen until it is too late. The better way is to eliminate the problem by keeping the cat away from it.

It's more practical to have shower doors than barriers placed in a tub that make the bathroom look a mess. A shower door can even be installed using silicone caulk (as used in structural applications, like fish aquariums). It can easily be removed without leaving any holes from screws.

🐾 ***Small Step Stool:*** This is ideal to have next to the toilet, because it makes it a lot easier for a cat to access. It's essential for a very young or

13

very old cat. Most stools are small enough to fit just nicely between a tub and toilet, making it out of the way, yet convenient for the kitty.

🐾 *Travel Kiddie Potty Seat:* I used this as an aid for smaller cats, 3-4-month-old kittens, cats that want to play in water, and cats that are afraid of water. It can also greatly help the "Furry-Footed".

A relatively new invention that can be bought online, the portable Travel Kiddie Potty Seat fits right on top of a regular seat and secures with suction cups. Get one that is as flat as possible, as opposed to curvy, and has more of a matte finish instead of being slick and glossy. Press it into place so it sticks well, and wet the cups if they become too dry and stop sticking. Even in a very dry climate, ours has still stuck extremely well!

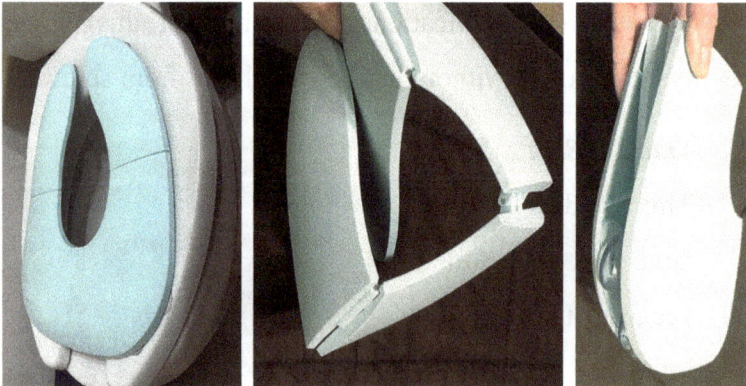

This makes the hole area smaller for "Water Lovers" and keeps them from going down to play in the water (as much). It can level out a slippery, curvy modern plastic seat. I put it backwards on the seat, which made the higher back the same level as the front.

These kiddie seats are nice. So easily cleanable, are easily removed with the provided little pry tool, and they fold up for storage or travel. Some have a storage pouch. It turned out to be a great purchase! I wish I had one years ago. It would have saved many cats from falling in.

🐾 🐾 🐾 🐾

Some Little Extras That Help a Lot

There are a few items that may be very nice to have. A lot of these items can be made yourself if you are handy, and we will cover in D.I.Y.s in the back Appendix.

🐾 ***Double Cat Toilet Seat:*** Not available commercially as yet, this consists of two seats and no lid, and is designed for the peaceful coexistence of humans and felines sharing the same toilet. The cat goes on the lower seat, and the human

can be easily adapted to accommodate older cats and the "Furry-Footed" by putting non-skid tape" (next entry) on the cat seat.

🐾 *Non-Skid Adhesive Tape:* Non-skid tape made in a clear soft rubber, is waterproof, cleanable, and designed for steps and showers. In the old days, it came as black sandpaper, and was horrible if you accidentally sat on it. The new clear tape comes in 2-3-inch-wide rolls, is not uncomfortable if you do sit on it, and provides just enough traction for furry paws. Cut it in triangular strips and stick on the seat. There is plenty enough left to have replacement tape on hand if needed.

🐾 *Removable Tub Cover:* If you don't have a shower door, try a removable tub cover. Some are pretty, and made as additional storage space for extra tubs. If you're handy, you can build one. This also came in handy once for a very different purpose, to keep a mother cat and her kittens safely contained in the tub!

🐾 *Portable Toilet:* If you have a limited number of toilets, and very young or very old occupants in the home that

16

"need to go now!", this may be a nice option. There are many places that sell these premade for campers and survivalists. It may just be worth it to purchase one. Handy cat lovers can probably even make their own.

🐾 ***Toilet Paper Guard:*** Only necessary if a cat has a habit of unrolling paper. Some types click onto the roll, most are wall-mounted. The free, no fuss alternative is to just turn the roll around and have it dispense backwards.

🐾 ***Clear Bleach Toilet Tank Tabs:*** Only needed if a cat regularly drinks out of toilet bowls. The strong smell deters this behavior. It still may not prevent a "Water Lover" or "Digger" from getting into the water. These types generally shake off any water, and don't tend to wash it off when it does get on their paws. The chlorine dissipates quickly, and is dilute enough to not cause any problems.

🐾 🐾 🐾 🐾

Items in Case of "Accidents"

🐾 Organic Baby Wipes and/or paper towels for cleanup of the cat (especially if they are longhairs) and your seat.

🐾 Sanitary Wipes for the floor, or occasional drip on the toilet seat.

🐾 A UV-A Black Light Flashlight will help you see accidents that may be invisible to the human eye, but is certainly not to the feline nose. This is great for pre-training cleanup. Urine and fecal matter glows when the light shines on it at a certain angle. It must be used in the dark, and fairly close up, or it won't work as well. Never look directly at the light, only what it is shining on.

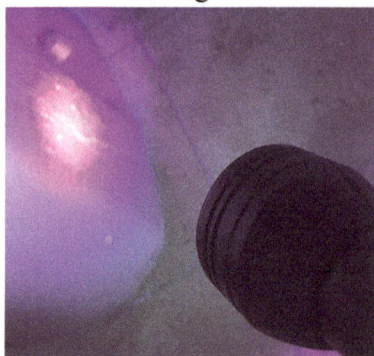

🐾 "Odor Mute™" in the pink box, that eliminates cat-detected scents. It's an enzyme product that has been around for 50 years, and even works for skunk odor. I don't usually see this in stores very often, so I thought I would include a picture. I have even used this to get rid of cat urine odors in porous concrete floors and grout. They say it has an 8-year shelf life, so it keeps.

Chapter 2

Training for Humans

What to Do, What Not to Do

It is as important to know what *not* to do, as it is to know what *to* do. Mental preparedness goes a long way in having training success. A lot of times when something is new, people have a fear of the unknown. This book should ideally help you be prepared for what could, should, and will happen (the cat learns to go on the potty, gradually, step by step). It can also give you an idea of what hopefully won't happen (accidents, failure) so that you can meet the challenge if it arises, and potentially correct it.

🐾 🐾 🐾 🐾

Think Like the Cat

For training to go really well, you have got to put yourself in the cat's place. Remember, it is a new thing going on, and cats don't usually like new changes. Change makes most cats nervous. You want to keep your cat calm and stress-free as possible. As the saying goes, "Do unto others as you would have them do to you", it is the same for the cat. Be patient with them, talk softly and calmly to them if they are visibly nervous. Cuddle with them and pet them. All this helps with bonding, and the more you are bonded with your cat, the better they will respond. They will want to please you and make you proud. For most cats, the training process will bring you even closer.

🐾 🐾 🐾 🐾

How You Should Behave

Cats understand human speech to some extent. Any time a certain pair of doves were out on the porch outside and the cats were watching I would say, "The birdies are out" or "There are the birdies!" One day, as I was in the living room and the cats were sound asleep in another room, the doves landed on the porch. I calmly said, "Oh... Birdies!" The cats came racing out of the room to look out at the porch. They will definitely come to know what you mean when you ask them, "Do you have to go potty?"

Repetition is good! "You can do it [Kitty's Name]". "Go potty get a treat!" This also goes well with a visual aid back and forth. Go potty (point to toilet) get treat (hold up treat bag).

When they do go, give that treat, lots of praise and attention, and tell them how proud you are of them. ("Good [boy/girl] [Name]!") It gives them confidence to know that they did the right thing.

Some very loyal cats that might worry about doing something wrong, may be afraid and not want to go, because they think it's in the wrong place (such as the sweet kitty who had to go to the vet to be relieved). You must reassure them that they are doing the right thing and it is just a little different than usual. The treat and praise backs this up in their minds, and the next time they won't worry and stress about it, they will just go.

🐾 🐾 🐾 🐾

Don't Panic and Be Calm

It is important that no matter what, you stay calm and in control of your own emotions. The first time they go in any phase is always hard and stressful. If you yell or threaten them, this is not going to help, and in fact will have the exact opposite effect of what you want. Yelling will only traumatize the cat, and ruins any chance of potty training. I always practice what I call "Tone of Voice Training". Speak to them calmly in a low voice. Loud noises can stress the cat out. Quick threatening gestures can scare them and they may run away.

If they threaten to go in the wrong place say in a calm low voice "No... no.". You can usually tell ahead of time if they are about to go. (See Weird Behaviors When A Cat Has to Go on page 42.) Generally, they will scratch around to prepare an area beforehand. Do not panic, and stay calm. If they do start to squat and go, gently pick them up from around their middle and place them on the toilet seat as they are going. Quickly pick up any poops that may have fallen (clean up the residue later, this is an extremely crucial time) and place the poops in the toilet or trainer pan. This sometimes is the very beginning of their actual understanding as to where they are supposed to go. When they are done, verbally praise them, show them what they did in the potty, tell them it is good, and follow up with a treat.

After a treat, I also show them again what they did. Depending on the phase they are in, I show them what happens to their "deposit". In early stages, I immediately clean out the litter and/or deposit from the trainer and place it in a disposable bag, saying "What a good baby!" If they are up to PHASES 3 or 4, I show them their deposit, flush the toilet, and say, "Good Baby, look at that! Down it goes!", both are followed up by more petting. They really connect what they are doing this way, and they feel good about what they have done.

Everyone Needs a Safe Place to Go

Just as most humans need to relax when they go, (read the paper or a book, etc.) the cat needs to be relaxed and have a safe place to go. Some humans can't stand public restrooms, it makes them nervous to use them. Well, with each new phase, it is for the cat like using that public restroom! And while we may have to use it on occasion, like it or not, that is how the cat feels too. For most cats, going "#2" is the harder part. (Probably for most humans too!) As long as they are comfortable, not interrupted, or distracted with a lot of noise or movement, they should find it easier to go. Keep the minimum of people around, and stay fairly quiet except for gentle coaching.

🐾 🐾 🐾 🐾

Keep Distractions to a Minimum!

This goes along with having a "safe" place to go. It is very important to make sure that the cat can concentrate on what they are doing, and not be distracted with toys, loud noises, lots of people, or other cats bothering them. The environment at first should be calm and quiet, with gentle human coaching. It may be a fascinating sight to watch at first, and to watch the progress, but keep extra people out of the bathroom and away so that they don't make noise.

No "Wrong Way" to Get the Job Done

Unless they are about to miss their "target", don't be nit-picky! If the cat sits on the toilet facing the tank or toward either side, it is not a problem! The seat is made for human posteriors, not cats. Maybe it is more ideal for a human to sit facing away from the tank, but only because that is how the seat is shaped.

Therefore, the cat can face any way they want to since they aren't truly sitting on the seat, but squatting or even sometimes standing to get into position. As long as a cat has his bottom over the hole and makes that target, there is no wrong way to go! If a Pet Parent makes too much of a fuss or is too critical, it is only going to make the cat nervous and insecure. If the cat is about to not make the target, gently slide them over until they are over the hole. Eventually they do find their comfortable footing/seating, and hey, if it is backwards, who cares?!

🐾 🐾 🐾 🐾

Quantity Versus Quality

Although generally humans tend to see this in the opposite light, with a cat, the more the repetition, the better, and the more ingrained an idea becomes. As has been said, they are creatures of habit, and our goal is to get them into the habit of going on the potty. So, what do I mean by quantity versus quality? During the PHASE 1, a cat may go in the trainer pan, perfectly positioned (quality). That may seem nice, but if the cat keeps avoiding doing that, it won't get "programmed" that this is what it should do. The more times the cat goes where they are supposed to (quantity), the more it gets ingrained.

Some cats are extremely stubborn, and will limit the number of times that they go to the bathroom. Some hold out until the absolute last possible minute, being obviously not looking too comfortable. For "#1" they may plop down and roll around on the floor. For "#2", they may race around the house, or get stimulated by playing with a toy. Eventually they have to give in, and will finally go. However, these stubborn types are prolonging their own training. One cat waited so long that he had to go to the vet to be relieved, but this was extremely unusual.

Ideally, they should go at least 7-10 times per phase, and get more comfortable each time they go. The more they go the more confident and relaxed they become.

🐾 🐾 🐾 🐾

Are They Ready for the Next Phase?

When the cat is no longer avoiding using the toilet or litter trainer, and has gone several times and comes to relax, they will start going on their own. Unless they are super intent on getting their treat, they often sneak in and go all by themselves just to prove that they can. This is when they have finally relaxed and accepted the change. A few more times of going on their own like this, and they are ready for the next phase. Ideally, they should have gone around 7-10 times if not more. On average about a week per phase (that equates to at least once a day for each way). Do not rush it though. A cat should not feel pressured, or it is just going to stress them out and they are more likely to fail. Let the kitty go at their own pace. When they seem happy and relaxed, approach the toilet with tail in the air and ears pointed up and forward, instead of ears back or tail drooping, they should be pretty confident.

🐾 🐾 🐾 🐾

Overview of the Training Process

The training process can be used for multiple cats, and always must go at the pace of the slowest one. A cat can never ever be rushed in its training, or it can ruin the chances of success. Of course, it all depends on the cat. Some are faster learners than others. It helps to treat each cat equally, with no outright favoritism. Each kitty must feel loved and important in their own right.

When I was a teenager and young adult, my mother and I had up to ten cats at once, and we took this concept to the extreme. Each cat his or her very own shelf or table to eat their food on, and we supervised them. This helped them to be more well-adjusted, without fear of other cats coming to steal their food, or be chased off. When feeding time came, it was an amazing sight to see when we called them to eat. Each cat would come running and go directly to their specific spot.

July of 1989 at Mum's Place: (Left-Right) Peanuts, TuffyNuff (top shelf), Cleo (below), Chessie, Toby, Junior, Arthur, Sweet P., Roddy, and Reggie.

The tradition continues in my own feline family to this day...

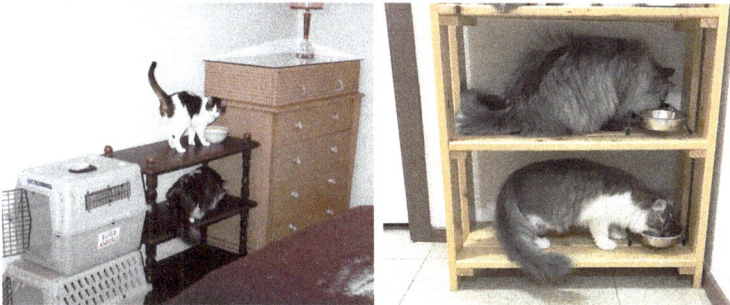

In 2000   (Top to Bottom)   **In 2020**
Loea and Sweet P.   Katerina and Frankie.

If there is a new additional cat that has already been socialized and is familiar with the rest of the cat family, the other cats will often help to train each other. If possible, let the new cat watch from afar in your arms (if they allow this). Visual reference can be a great help!

Be prepared, during potty training, there may be accidents. If it happens too frequently, it can be problematic. If only occasional, it may not be a total "deal breaker". If a cat urinates where they shouldn't, this is a much harder case to deal with and possibly may be an indication that this cat is not going to cooperate. I had only two cases of cats that did this. One went in my craft supplies (very much out of reach and not in a comfortable place to go). He was an "Arrogant Cat", who ruled over everyone and had brains too. Another "Top Cat" type that did this years later made it even more personal. She would get up on my bed at night, come up on my stomach and squat. After three different occasions of this, it was enough.

🐾 🐾 🐾 🐾

Teaching a Cat Right from Wrong

Some cats have more of a conscience than others, depending on their personality type. Those more loyal and obedient kitties that do have a conscience will likely want to make you proud and do the right thing. On a side note, here are some general behavioral correction tips that I have found to be very successful.

First, if a cat is new to a household, (or sometimes those personality types that just like to try to), they *are going to test you*. Just remember that by "testing" you, just as with little human kids, it is a form of learning what is right and wrong. How else would they know if something is wrong unless they are taught that it is?

If a cat is being very bad, or doing something it shouldn't, I first say "No... no", in a low calm voice. If they continue, I say "No!", "stop it", or "get down" in a little sharper tone. If they persist doing what they shouldn't, or repeat a bad behavior, I have an almost siren-like (very obnoxious) "Ooohh?!" call that I do, and then I take a spray bottle filled with water and squirt them on the spot. This has worked exceptionally well for cats attempting to jump onto a dining table or kitchen counter. I use it only as a last resort, and *never* use it for potty training. I only have to do it once or twice, and they get the message loud and clear. My cats have been extremely well behaved.

Once taught, (or twice if they aren't very bright), they usually get the concept, and don't continue the offensive behavior, because they know they are going to get a squirt from the "Big Bad Spray Bottle", and an obnoxious "Oooh Siren".

As for behavioral correction during potty training, when in the bathroom, only use a calm low voice to say "No", and stay as calm as possible. Never use the squirting or "Ooohh Siren".

When they do good, always praise and give treats-without fail. This backs up the happy feeling that they did well and pleased you. If they happen to have gone in the potty and you discover it later, still praise them and acknowledge it. They know and remember what they did.

Chapter 3

Feline Psychology 101

What Makes Your Cat "Tick"

It is so important to really know and understand your cat and their unique personality and traits. Every individual and their traits must be taken into consideration in order to help make the cat's training successful. Fortunately, this is not such a difficult task, when you know their particular needs. That is why there is a whole section called "Assessing A Cat's Traits for Training", dedicated to different personality traits, temperaments and physical circumstances.

It's also very helpful for your cat to be so close with you that you are viewed as "one of the cats". You can be a "Top Cat", and let the other cats know that you mean business, but the more "equal" they view you the better. Cats are dignified creatures, and do not like to be considered inferior. When you are their "equal", a "fellow cat", they respond with having more love and respect for you, and tend to develop a closer relationship with you. They usually behave better, and may give you the honor of grooming you like another cat. This is where it is ideal to be considered a "Pet Parent", where you take care of each other. Most of my closest cats loved to wash my face, and would happily let me comb them, enjoying every minute of it. This mutual trust and love would also allow me to clip their claws or administer medicine, because they realized that I was trying to help them, and would never hurt them in any way.

🐾 🐾 🐾 🐾

How Cats Think

Any cat person knows that if anything, you do not own a cat, they own you! (And of course, we view it as being a privilege!) Therefore, we shall refer to the humans in charge as the "Pet Parents". Your relationship with your cat or kitten should ideally be that close. Although just as with human parents and their children, if you live in a multi-cat household, favoritism should not be allowed with feline children either. All should be treated equally, even if you do happen to be closer to one cat than another. Every cat needs to feel important and loved. Jealousy of other cats can potentially interfere with training.

You need to look at the training process as something beneficial from the cat's perspective, not something that *you* want the cat to do. They are very logical creatures, so consistent behavior on your part is essential. Routinely praise them and give them their special "Potty Treat" reward so that they know it pleased you. If they had gone in the potty earlier and you only discover it later, acknowledge that you saw it, praise them while showing them what they did, and give their treat. They will proudly remember.

Throughout this book, we refer to the human trainers in charge as the "Pet Parents". Your relationship with your cat or kitten should ideally be that close. Although just as with human parents and their children, if you live in a multi-cat household, favoritism should not be allowed with feline children either. All should be treated equally, even if you do happen to be closer to one cat than another. Every cat needs to feel important and loved. Jealousy of other cats can potentially interfere with training.

🐾 🐾 🐾 🐾

Feline Body Language

Although cats can have hundreds of different linguistic characteristics that vary greatly, most cats tend to share the same universal body language. It is indicative of their mood and thought process. Knowing how to "read" your cat, can help you with adjusting the potty training to fit their specific needs, and evaluate how they are dealing with it psychologically. (Are they stressed out? Are they accepting it happily?) Since they cannot put their emotions into words, a cat's body language speaks for them.

Note: The very photogenic baby Katerina has "volunteered" to demonstrate various facial expressions and body language. She can appear quite ferocious during play attack mode, but rest assured, she was never provoked or forced to pose. Every picture in this book was natural and of each cat's own volition.

🐾 *Happy Cats:* Although it is perhaps the most commonly-known trait of a happy cat, purring is not necessarily a sign of feline happiness! The more telltale signs are in the body language- the cat's eyes are bright and attentive, their ears are held forward and upright, and the biggest indicator is that their tails will be held straight up in the air (many hold them straight up with the tips pointing down slightly like a question mark).

When not in the air, they may be very gently swaying their tail. When very excited, their whiskers will be flared out toward the front. Depending on their character traits and affection levels, they may rub against your legs, give you a "hug" with their tail, "Feline Kiss" you by rubbing their cheek gently against you (a form of loving possession), close their

eyes contentedly, and they may knead. Some kitties may even groom you if you are very close. One of the most common things that cat lovers know is the "Love Blink", where as they look at you with love in their eyes, they slowly close their eyes and open them, facing you the whole time. Happy cats will often knead on soft things like a pillow or bed, or on your lap. Hopefully throughout all stages of training, your kitty will remain happy, because they are experiencing it with plenty of love and patience.

🐾 ***Angry Cats:*** A cat that is mad is likely to be hyper-alert to any little sound or movement, have their heads darting

back and forth looking out for danger. Their eyes may be wide open, possibly with enlarged pupils and blink at you once quickly. Their ears are back, held closely against their head, with tail thrashing wildly back and forth, sometimes puffed out. They may move very slowly walking in almost in a crouching position, and then suddenly run away. If they growl, hiss, or arch their back with hair standing on end, you may not want to mess with them. They are warning you to get away, or they may scratch you.

🐾 *Nervous Cats:* Some stressed cats may be more docile during potty training, but can tend to get diarrhea or have blood in their stool due to intestinal irritation. It is normal for most cats to be a little nervous when starting their training, especially at PHASE 3, but hopefully this won't last long. If you are patient and gentle with them, they may just relax a little.

🐾 *Wary Cats:* Usually the more intellectual the cat, the more wary they can be. They have their own set of body language cues. They often hold one of their front paws up. (I still haven't figured out the logic to this.) Their tip of their tail will twitch quickly. Sometimes, they will hold one ear back and the other ear toward the front. (Most likely an aid to listening for danger.) If a cat's ears could signify a human's eyebrows, it would be the same as one eyebrow up and the other down.

🐾 ***Scaredy Cats:*** A timid, scared cat is easily stressed out, but they are not likely to lash out at anyone. They are likely to be alert and jumpy at any little sound or movement, their eyes will be fearful open wide, possibly with pupils enlarged, ears may be back slightly, and the tail is tucked closely to the cat's body or between its legs. They may tremble or shiver if they are extremely frightened, which is more common if it is a new cat in a new place. They are usually very quiet, and hide a lot, sometimes getting into places that you never dreamed were possible. They may stop eating and drinking.

🐾 ***Depressed Cats:*** Sad or depressed cats may be lethargic, very quiet, hide or seek warmth, and may stop eating, drinking, or even going to the litter box. Sometimes, they may even eliminate outside of the litter box. I have not experienced this during my cats

being toilet trained, but there are some general signs of depression. The eyes are dull and maybe the "third eyelid" (nictitating membrane) is up. (This can also be a sign of having a fever.) The tail is held low, possibly dragging on the floor, or even between the legs. The ears may be back. They may curl up in a corner, not want to be petted, or stay under the bed or a place where they won't be bothered. They may seek out a warm spot for comfort. A depressed cat is a very sad sight to see, and you never want your cat to get this way. You should keep an eye on them, just to make sure that the cat isn't sick, because the symptoms can be similar.

🐾 🐾 🐾 🐾

Tale of Tails

Cats may pet you with their tail, or give you a gentle little "tail hug" as they walk by. If you are standing there, they may even wrap their tail around your legs as though to tenderly put their arm around you. Aside from this sweet gesture, have you ever noticed that cats tend to have no idea where their tails are at any given time?

This is perhaps why kittens chase their tails, because they don't even recognize that these are part of their own body! It is often evident when a cat turns around and sticks their tail in their food. Sometimes they may whop you in the face with it if they are standing on a desk in front of you, or getting cozy with you in a bed.

The tail can also sometimes make for a little problem on the potty, depending on the cat. When they go, each has

their own particular posture. Some may stand on their tip toes, others jump up and down with their front legs while sitting on the seat, and yet another may hold up one front paw.

Their unique tail "signature" is the same way. Most cats hold their tails in an inverted arch as they go, like a "U", as in Loea's picture above. This is a very good posture, as the tail stays out of the way the whole time. Some cats (like Katerina on the cover), merely rest their tails on the seat and let them dangle over the edge. That is not problematic unless the cat is small and their tail goes down into the toilet. There are cats that arch their tails upward like a rainbow. This is not so great. Sometimes if it is a tighter radius in nearly a perfect circle, they can end up going on the tip of their tail. Even worse, there are cats that have long tails, and not knowing where they are, drape them

39

through the hole and they go down in the water. Perhaps the most common position is the cat who holds its tail straight out. This is a very good position, as it clears the toilet water and the deposit throughout the whole deed.

Once potty training is completed, a multi-cat household can have occasional "Traffic Jams", in which more than one cat wants to go at the same time, and sometimes on the same seat! In this scenario, one cat may end up going on another cat's tail. This is highly unusual, but can happen. Once a cat is comfortable going, you can usually intervene and move the other cat's tail out of the way.

🐾 🐾 🐾 🐾

What's Going On When They Do the Deed

Interestingly enough, cats will rarely go both "#1" and "#2" at the same time, and generally do them each in different potty sessions. There is no set "rule" for how their eliminations will occur. Sometimes they will go "#1" first, other times they will do it after "#2". Each cat is different.

After PHASES 2 or 3 of training, a cat may hold his urine and refuse to go until it simply can't take it anymore. Some cats will wait 24-36 hours. Any more than that can be serious, and the cat may have to go to the vet to get relieved, although this is not very common. When the cat is about ready to burst", they will usually drop to the ground and roll around. Keep putting them on the potty and show them where to go. They will go eventually. Most kitties don't have as much of a problem with going "#1".

Many cats have more trouble adjusting to going "#2", perhaps because it takes a lot more muscles to get the job done.

Several things are happening when they pass a stool. First, they must make sure they are not in a situation where they can be threatened by predators (A Safe Place to Go), since they are very vulnerable and almost helpless when they are in the act of going. Next, they must get into their favored position. Potty-trained cats have some extra steps to go through. They must make sure they hit the desired target (the hole or water below), balance carefully on the seat, and push, all at the same time. This can be an enormous strain at first. Some cats are so stressed that they may even develop mucus or a small amount of blood at the end of their stool. While this can be extremely alarming, it may not be too much of a concern unless it happens more than a few times. If it does persist, take the cat to the vet, as it could be a sign of a serious illness. Most likely, it will clear up after a few times as they relax.

Other cats find it fairly easy, and cheerfully accommodate the new phase. Typically, these cats will hop up on the seat, get into position, start to go, and some may jump up slightly with their front legs (kind of like a dog sitting up and begging). The added "leverage" helps them push it out.

A sign cats may have to go is they will run around wildly, or play vigorously with a toy. These things seem to help stimulate them to go. As said before, show them where to go, and they will go eventually. More odd actions are discussed below.

🐾 🐾 🐾 🐾

Weird Behaviors When a Cat Has to Go

When cats are in their stubborn mode putting off going to the bathroom, they can exhibit some pretty strange behaviors. Most often, when they feel the urge to go either way coming on, they will refuse to eat. They simply don't feel like it. They may get nauseous, or feel full already. They may meow for you to come and watch them. As they are waiting, they show certain signs of what they need to do. For "#1", they may pace around, suddenly drop to the floor, and then roll around. This is likely in effort to get their minds off of going, and kind of equivalent to a human "dancing around" if they have to go but don't want to go yet.

When putting off "#2", cats may race around the house like crazy, run and jump on things, or shoot up the side of their cat tree and then jump down. They may suddenly start playing very violently with a favorite toy. Others decide to nibble on food, but this is not nearly as common. These things can take their minds off of going, but sometimes too, it is a way of getting stimulated to go. At this stage in their "game", they must be supervised. Occasionally they will have waited too long and it just starts coming whether they like it or not.

As they are considering going, they may start exploring areas near the toilet. (This is what the suggested barriers prevent.) When they are really about to go, they will start sniffing the floor closely, meowing a lot, or start digging at the bathroom floor next to the toilet, or even a bit away from it, but in the same room. Digging at the floor is usually a bad sign, because that really gets them stimulated to go, and soon!

🐾 🐾 🐾 🐾

Pre-Potty Cat "Rituals"

Pre-potty cat rituals can take place in a variety of ways, usually accompanied by a lot of pitiful meowing...

The Shuffle: Some kitties have a rather cute habit of jumping on the seat, and as they perch, they will shuffle their hind feet back and forth and side to side, until they get just the right footing. Then they go just fine and perfectly perched. Junior was known to do this, and would quietly "talk" as he got into place.

Wild Scratching: Less common, there are kitties who will jump up on the seat and wildly scratch at it, ears back concentrating very hard, rump in the air, and front legs outstretched. They may circle a few times too. Suddenly at the last minute when they can hold it no longer, they quickly get into position and go. Most likely, this ritual gets them stimulated to go by all of the scratching, and is a substitute for their litter. These kitties are highly likely to be "Diggers", and would normally kick their litter out of the box.

Jump Up, Down, and All Around*:* Some cats have a ritual of jumping onto the toilet seat and circling a few times, then jumping down, then getting back up. They may even get into perfect position a few times, then jump down just when you think they are finally going to go. Some cats just automatically do this at any stage, and others will still do it even after training. Jump up on the seat, get down. Jump up, walk around a bit, get down. They repeat it so many times you would think they would get dizzy! Then after all that fuss, they may walk away and then go take a nap or play. It leaves one wondering, "Hmm, did they possibly go do their deed somewhere else in the house where they shouldn't have and I just didn't see it?"

It is a bizarre, yet normal occurrence. Cats new to potty can simply lose the sensation of having to go, or decide to just wait and try again later when the next "wave" hits. Then the ritual starts all over again. Eventually they will go, and most likely where they should. It is extremely important to supervise them at these early stages, because you don't want them to go somewhere in the wrong place.

This behavior usually occurs at the start of each phase, so get used to it! Usually, most cats will meow a lot before they go, which helps warn you ahead of time. Just as long as you stay with them, they should be okay. I can't think of a single cat in training that has not done some sort of ritual.

🐾 🐾 🐾 🐾

Different Methods for Specific Cats

Different strategies can be used for different cats. The same method can be used for cats who like water and are afraid of water. The general idea is to have the hole small enough that the cat won't go down into the toilet bowl. The Water Lover may want to play in the water below, and the Water Hater is afraid of falling in because the hole is too large, especially if they are young or small. For both of these, I recommend an auxiliary Travel Kiddie Potty Seat that fits on top of the seat. It makes the hole much smaller, so the desired outcome of not getting into the water is the same. Eventually it can be removed.

Adapt training to the cat's personality and physical traits. Each cat may be different, but there are usually ways to compromise.

FROM 1971-1984 (Left to Right)
SNIP, MARMALADE (w/ Moppett to left),
TUMBLEWEED "KITTY", CHESSIE,
TUFFYNUFF, SPECIAL LADY,
PEANUTS, and CLEO.

Chapter 4

Assessing Cat Traits for Training

How Well Will My Cat Train?

There are varying circumstances that make a cat fit for potty training, such as temperament, intelligence, age, personality, and physical condition. These are some of the traits that can make or break potty training. The best "students" are spayed and neutered, since unaltered cats have hormones and the urge to mark their territory.

Aside from any hormonal factors, many personality and physical traits can be identified, and one or several different traits can apply to one single kitty.

There are a few that tend to go along with other similar traits, but since each and every cat is a unique individual with their own background experiences, it helps to make up their specific psychological profile.

Let us examine each of twenty-five different personality and physical traits in detail, and hopefully it will help allow you to know your cat, and how to deal with them better.

It can only help you to see things more clearly from their point of view.

Cat Traits in Detail

In alphabetical order, here are twenty-five of the most common feline traits...

The Affectionate Cat

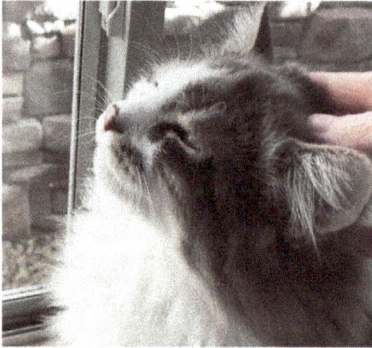

Usually, the more loving and affectionate the cat, the more likely they are to want to please you. They should have a very easy time with potty training. Give them lots of extra petting and praise every time they successfully go. Some affectionate cats have more of a drive for loving attention than for food treats. They benefit most from you taking your time with them and staying there throughout their "potty session". Talk to them gently and reassuring them that you love them and it will make you happy if they go potty in the toilet.

You can pet them occasionally as they are on the potty or trainer, but do not pet them *too much*. Some very affectionate cats can become overly excited with the petting and it can have the opposite effect, distracting them from what they are supposed to be doing. Give them a petting/cuddling session after they are done going potty, and that can even be part of their motivational "potty treat".

The Arrogant Cat

This personality type has a huge ego, is usually highly intelligent, and they know it! They may occasionally be potty-trainable, but they are usually best kept as a single-cat in a household, showered with his or her own love and attention all to themselves. If they do not accept potty training, you may have to keep them using a litter box, or they are likely to rebel and eliminate in a very bad place where they know you don't want them to go. Some Arrogant Cats can be very spiteful as well. I have had much less luck training Arrogant Cats. They are naturally defiant,

thinking they are too good and smart for it, refusing to be trained to do tricks like a "lowly" dog. No, they are independent and self-taught.

Many Arrogant Cats are also mentally unhealthy "Top Cats" that like to terrorize other cats of a "lower" (in their eyes) status. Nobody is safe from "the attitude". Even humans who hate cats will be challenged by an Arrogant Cat who will either give them the "stare down", or be "in their face" to flaunt their superior status. Arthur (pictured above) was so arrogant, that a hard flick on the nose (that had to have hurt!) from a cat-hating boss didn't even faze him. He just kept pestering the boss during our meeting until he eventually left when it was over. The Arrogant Cat can be potty-trained, only if they believe they benefit from it. Whatever this may be, must be directly determined by the "Pet Parent" after much observation as to what motivates this cat to do certain things.

🐾 🐾 🐾 🐾

The Close Cat

Probably the total opposite of the Arrogant Cat, the Close Cat is just about inseparable from their Pet Parent.

The cat and human have complete trust, love and respect for each other, and the cat won't suspect the human of any agenda. The closer a cat, the easier and more willing they are to be trained. You should have no trouble training them at all. Much like the Affectionate Cat, they aim to please, but due to a slightly different motivation.

Whereas the Affectionate Cat craves the attention and physical petting, the Close Cat, may not always be quite so outwardly affectionate. Their motivation is to just be with the Pet Parent, please them, and like to know that they are appreciated in return. Often, the Close Cat will sleep with the Pet Parent, can sometimes get jealous of other cats getting too much attention from the Pet Parent, and will usually be found somewhere in the same room as the Pet Parent. They may even follow the Pet Parent around the house, tagging along where ever they go, and "helping" with whatever they are doing such as folding laundry or cleaning.

The Close Cat may respond to a variety of treats, whether physical petting or cuddling, food treats, or a combination. They often get confidence to use the potty with simple "Love Blinks", kind words of encouragement, and of course, the Pet Parent's presence during the "potty sessions".

🐾 🐾 🐾 🐾

The Confident Cat

Not at all to be confused with the "Arrogant Cat", this personality type is simply very well-adjusted and happy. They have such a wonderful attitude, they don't let anything bother them, and do not hold a grudge like many cats can. They know that they are loved, and they love their Pet Parents. They take problems in stride, and still have a bubbly cheerfulness about them. They don't have a spiteful bone in their body, and some communicate verbally or with physical or visual cues. There should be no issues with potty training, and it should go very well. The Confident Cat can be motivated by food treats or play time, depending on what the cat likes the most.

This type is very confident in everything they do, viewing potty training as being just a fun challenge. They learn very quickly and easily. One Confident Cat had her share of challenges with allergies and diarrhea, but these were not viewed as obstacles, and she made it through just fine. She was finally able to get on a food that was suited for her special needs and was fine after that. Still, she achieved her potty graduation with grace and pride, despite her hardships which she could have very easily complained about. Complaint is simply not in the Confident Cat's "vocabulary".

🐾 🐾 🐾 🐾

The Declawed Cat

Don't get me started on the topic of declawing a cat! Amputating the ends of one's toes so that the cat no longer can use its natural scratching and climbing abilities, or defend itself from predators, is not a good thing in any circumstances. I highly doubt that a declawed cat would be suitable to be potty-trained, as it could possibly affect their balance. It is not unheard of for a declawed cat to potentially quit going in their litter box for that matter, and have moderate to severe psychological problems. (I have no picture, because I would never have a cat declawed.)

The Digger

This type of cat can be potty-trained, but it can be quite hard for them. The Digger loves to sit in the litter box scratching and digging, digging and scratching, sometimes so ferociously that they throw the litter right out of their box. They simply love to scratch around and dig. It is a stimulation that helps enable them to go. They need this stimulus, and when they don't have the litter to scratch at anymore, it can make them upset. They may also be the type to continue covering up their business after they are done, in the same manner in which they started. Fortunately, most "Diggers" will continue scratching at the trainer pan or the toilet seat.

The only a problem is if the Digger is also a "Sloppy Cat", who doesn't care at all if they get into their own excrement, violently digging afterwards too. If they continue to dig and scratch after they are finished, try to shoo them off of the seat and side track them with their treat. It may be a wise idea to invest in a Kiddie Travel Potty Seat to place on top and keep them from going down into the toilet bowl, just as for the "Water Lover".

The Disciplined Cat

The Disciplined Cat can be an extremely "Stubborn Cat", but can still be a very good candidate for training. The Disciplined Cat will hold it and refuse to go for sometimes 36 hours. One such cat is Katerina, (left) who is without a doubt the most disciplined (I would even say "OCD") kitty that I have ever seen in my life. She created her own time schedule, and made up (taught me) exactly how she wanted her food. And at what consistency, and what time she would eat it. She made her own potty schedule, even as a kitten back when she had a normal litter box. When she first came to me, she refused to go for the first 36 hours. Then, it was every 24 hours like clockwork. Once settled in, she would go "#1" and "#2" in the morning, and that was it. This was even before training for the toilet!

The Disciplined Cat knows exactly what she wants and how she wants it. They are very well behaved, but everything has to be just a certain way. It took many months, but now Katerina goes "#1" twice a day, once in the morning and once at night, and "#2" usually once in the morning. Rarely will she deviate. She is happy getting a food treat, but if she goes in the guest bathroom, the treat must be given on the counter in that bathroom. If she goes where she prefers in my bathroom, the treat must be given in the Master bathroom sink. There is no other way in her mind!

The Disciplined Cat must be taught who is in charge, otherwise they will not budge from their position. Once they are broken (somewhat) of their rigidity, they will comply much easier. Katerina was the longest training student in my history at a solid 4 months if not slightly longer, but still would tend to go "#2" on the floor next to the toilet at times. This was usually due to having harder stools that probably were too uncomfortable. (This was aided by adding extra water to her food.) Plus, she kept insisting that she wanted to use the challenging curvy modern slippery toilet. I finally (literally) closed the door on that habit. Next, she didn't want to use her brother's baby seat and turned up her nose. (She was a big girl now!) Once the baby seat was removed, she would go on the regular toilet seat. Fortunately, after these subtle little compromises, she has been going just fine on a specially made Double Cat Toilet Seat for the "Furry-Footed". It is much more comfortable and relaxed, especially since her little brother finally outgrew the baby seat.

The Fastidious Cat

This personality type is definitely a plus! The "Fastidious Cat" doesn't like to get their paws dirty. They don't dig in the litter to go, and do not tend to bury their deposits, in favor of just leaving the area as quickly as they can. This type of cat was *made* for potty training, and is usually far happier being toilet trained. My best student so far, Frankie trained in 27 days, and never had a single accident or threatened to go anywhere he shouldn't. He has several other combined traits as well, but his fastidiousness, and always keeping his privates clean (and trying to bury them if they weren't) really made his potty training easier.

🐾 🐾 🐾 🐾

The Furry-Footed

Not much needs to be expounded upon here. These are medium to long-haired cats, who have so much fur on the bottoms of their feet and between their

paw pads that they have a very hard time gripping onto the seat, and can slide right into the toilet bowl. Such a traumatic event could ruin potty training before it started! The good news is the Furry-Footed Cat is completely trainable, but they simply need a little bit more in the way of extra assistance. Depending on the cat's temperament and amount of fur, you can carefully trim around their paw pads with a tiny moustache scissors. (This is best done when they are sleepy or napping.) If their fur grows very fast, it may not be worth the time and trouble unless they actually enjoy this type of grooming. It is important to make sure they are combed well, because if a longhair gets mats, it can pull on their fur and it can hurt them as they jump up on the seat or try to balance. That can really interfere with potty training!

It is helpful to use a Travel Kiddie Potty Seat for extra surface area to perch on. (Although, this is more ideal for smaller cats. A large cat may not fit well and could miss the target.

Another option is to put clear rubber non-skid tape on your toilet seat. Lastly, make a Double Cat Toilet Seat with the non-slip tape or even more abrasive gritty non-slip on the bottom cat seat only. Aside from slippage, they usually train well, perhaps due to being closer to their Pet Parents. At least half of my potty-trained cats have been "Furry-Footed".

57

The Good Cat

Similar to the Obedient Cat, this personality type aims to please, is very cooperative, and puts up with a lot. They are good-natured as well as well-behaved. All of these qualities make for an easily potty trainable kitty. They may like to have physical playtime or cuddling instead of food treats, it all depends on the cat of course. They also usually will respond very well to verbal coaxing, especially when they are told they are good.

🐾 🐾 🐾 🐾

The Intelligent Cat

This cat type "gets" the concept of potty training. They usually exhibit very logical behavior, and teach themselves to do activities that will benefit them, such as opening cabinet doors or playing interactive games. These cats often breeze through training quickly and stay trained like it is totally natural for them.

On occasion, if a cat is exceedingly intelligent, it might just backfire, because they figure out what you want them to do, know that you want them to do it, but they don't want to cooperate. Usually, they will give in in the end.

The Intelligent Cat will often respond better to physical interactive playtime instead of treats as a reward.

🐾 🐾 🐾 🐾

The Liar

Almost every cat at the start of training has been a "Liar" at one time or another. It may only "lie to you" once, but they are merely testing you to what they can get away with. It is a natural thing, and doesn't mean they are bad. The cat acts like it has gone when it really hasn't. Some may even take credit for another cat's potty. That is when supervision comes in handy, plus knowing what each cat's deposits look like. They may be cheerful and meow at you, and even try to cover up or bury their "imaginary" deposit. Once in a while, treat-driven cats will "fake it", and the only way to make sure if they are "telling the truth", is to check the litter pan, trainer tray, or toilet very carefully. If there is absolutely nothing there, (no damp or clumpy litter in the trainer box, not even slightly yellow water or disintegrated crumbs in the toilet), explain to them that they "actually have to go potty in order to get their treat", and you are wise to their little charade. Most cats will give up and continue living an "honest" life. Some may try to fake it a few more times. Just stick to checking, and making sure that they are not telling the truth, and if they are lying, do not give that treat for any reason! If they do turn out to be honest and have actually gone where they should, shower them with treats and attention. Fortunately, most grow out if this "stage". Since it is temporary, there's no example picture, because everyone has done it, and all have stopped.

🐾 🐾 🐾 🐾

The Nervous/Insecure Cat

A Nervous/Insecure Cat may refuse to go until it is nearly too late. If they persist in being so nervous that they refuse to go, it may not be a healthy choice to have them be toilet trained. You may want to postpone training until a later time. Fortunately, even nervous, insecure cats can learn the potty flawlessly with enough love and attention. You must stay with them almost constantly throughout their first eliminations, especially during PHASE 4 and graduation. Make absolutely sure that everything is calm and quiet with no distractions, loud noises, or other stresses. This is a very stressful time for the Nervous/Insecure Cat. Talk to them gently and reassure them that what they are doing is good. This way they will relax, and it will help correct any potential errors, like going on the floor. (See "Starting to Go in the Wrong Place" on page 94.) The main thing is to make sure they do eventually go. Once they do, shower them with affection and treats to show that they did well.

🐾 🐾 🐾 🐾

The Not-So-Bright Cat

Sometimes having a Not-So-Bright Cat can actually be a plus, because the cat is trained more through its desire for the treat. They are more on the "robotic" side, and realize through lots of repetition, they will get what they want.

More often than not, the Not-So-Bright Cat is an excellent student for potty training. Consistency is the key to their learning, and most often their favorite reward is food treats. Make sure to always give that treat right after they go. Make sure to catch them in the act of going, so that if it is in the wrong place it is corrected immediately, or if they do go where they should, give that treat!

Keep this up, and they may just graduate ahead of the Intelligent Cat. It is actually pretty typical.

The Obedient Cat

This kitty is a people-pleaser. When it comes to something new in their life, they are always very concerned about doing what they should at all times, and/or fear that they may do something wrong. They may refuse to go to the bathroom at all until it is nearly too late. Junior, who afterwards was flawlessly toilet trained, at first refused to go and after 2 days had to be taken to the vet to be "squeezed out"! He required personal time and soothing speech, being reassured that he was doing the right thing. It is especially important that males are encouraged to go, so they don't develop dangerous blockages from crystals. Junior proved to be just fine, but having had another male cat die of cystitis as a child, I did not want to take any chances.

The Obedient Cat thrives on praise and attention, which builds their confidence and reassures them. They may be in it for the attention or the treat. Shower them with both as soon as they go where they should in all of the various phases. Once they do learn, they will not deviate from the toilet for the rest of their life, as long as they can help it!

62

The Obese Cat

I don't mean just slightly overweight; I am talking a truly "Obese" Cat by medical standards. I've never had one, so there is no picture example. However, I have had the sad misfortune to see them. These poor creatures, meant to be sleek and athletic, have become what appears to be more like a furry, oval balloon with four feet and a tail sticking out. It is a truly a crime to let a cat get like this!

Toilet training is never recommended for an Obese Cat. A heavy cat cannot move easily, is not agile enough to jump up and down, and can't balance properly. These things are a *must* for any toilet trained cat. If an Obese Cat were to try, they could potentially get severely injured or traumatized by falling into the toilet. Being overweight is not healthy for the cat either. An obese cat will eventually develop health problems, just like any human. A good diet and exercise help to keep cats trim and at the peak of health. Until the Obese Cat has lost all the pounds needed to be at their ideal weight, do not even attempt to potty train them. A qualified veterinarian should be consulted for dietary guidance, and the cat should get regular exercise, preferably with mutual, interactive play. It will ultimately help the cat and Pet Parent bond closer together. As I say throughout, close bonding helps immensely with potty training.

The Older Cat

The Older Cat is still very trainable, maybe even more so than a younger cat. Unless they have some sort of severe health problem, there is no reason *not* to try to train them. They are usually calmer, trusting, much more bonded with you, and usually want to please and do the right thing.

If they are starting to have problems with mild arthritis, make sure to keep a stool next to the toilet so they don't have to jump up so far. You may even want to make a "Double Cat Toilet Seat", and put non-slip tape on the cat's seat. This helps keep them from slipping if they just aren't that agile anymore. A "Furry-Footed" Cat may be young and still have trouble slipping off a seat, how much more so for the elder cat. Indeed, it was for an older already potty-trained 17-year-old cat that the Double Cat Toilet Seat was created for. She was Furry-Footed, and starting to get mild arthritis, so she wasn't getting up on the seat as easily. Accompanied by a stool next to the toilet, the double seat worked like a charm for 4 more years, and she happily went on the potty until shortly before her death.

The Sick Cat

Unless they have already been trained to go on the toilet, it may not be a good idea to train a new cat that is sick. Depending on the health problem, one should consider all issues. If a cat is weak and not feeling well, it is just more stress to add and will likely make the cat even unhealthier. If the cat has already been trained, and is simply getting older and sicker, it is a tough call. I had two cats that were potty-trained, but were experiencing severe illness, like kidney failure. These cats sincerely wanted

to go on the toilet! If this is the case, *not* having them go on the toilet can be a stressor. Consider Loea (above) who was diagnosed with Cardiomyopathy. As long as she was on her heart medicine, she continued to do extremely well on the potty.

Each individual cat must be decided upon on an individual, case by case basis. If an illness affects a cat's ability to balance, jump, have a normal bowel movement, etc., then it may just be time to revert back to a litter box for their health's sake and peace of mind. Unless a cat is so attached to the toilet, having gone on it for the bulk of its life, then something like custom made cat diapers may be a good way to go if they simply can't make it on the potty anymore. Such was the case with the two sick cats.

The Sloppy Cat

The Sloppy Cat often may also be a "Digger". This type doesn't care if they scratch around in their own excrement, get it on their paws, track it around, etc. Being a Sloppy Cat doesn't necessarily disqualify them from potty training; in fact, it might just help them to become tidier as time goes by.

It is less ideal if they try to dig down inside the toilet bowl, or even in the water itself to try to cover up their deed. Whether in litter or water, they may get their front paws, claws and back feet or tail into their deposit after they are done. Initial training may be rough and messy, but they may just prove to be a very good candidate in the end. Keep them tidy by cleaning their paws, and still give them a treat for going. This will help sidetrack them from burying their "treasure". If they continue trying to go into the water to cover their deposit, a Travel Kiddie Potty Seat, would restrict the hole size and help prevent them from going down into the bowl. A Sloppy Cat may get out of this habit altogether as time goes by, and the Kiddie Seat can eventually be removed. It is all in making certain actions a habit, and the more repetition the better.

The Spiteful Cat

This trait is totally unsuitable for potty training. They rebel, get even, and eliminate where they shouldn't on purpose just to be mean. They are often sprayers, and won't even try to go where they should. A Spiteful Cat may not even use a litter box.

Although, elimination outside of the toilet or litter box can possibly be a sign of illness, there is a vast difference. A sick cat may be in pain as they go, and they associate that with the area where they experienced the pain. They logically seek out a safe place to go where they think there won't be any pain. They will likely be looking down, or have their eyes closed. The Spiteful Cat is far different. They may look you straight in the eye as they go, and often choose to go on an item that they know is important to you. The worst scenario is if the cat actually goes *on you*!

Peanuts (above) was never tried on potty training. He had enough troubles with spraying, and would be classified as a "difficult" cat. As a very young male, the first time he ever sprayed was in my eye as he jumped above me on the couch. Sadly, that was the start of a lifelong a bad habit.

67

The Stubborn Cat

This trait can be fairly common. They are trainable, but it often takes the Stubborn Cat a little longer than most to train. Similar to the Arrogant Cat, they may feel that such a thing is "beneath their dignity". The difference is, that they aren't driven as much by their ego, as much as simply wanting to do things the way they like to do them.

Make sure to find an irresistible treat that they just can't refuse. The Potty Treat has to be worth their "expended effort" in order to comply. Once you gain their confidence that they know they will be rewarded, a Stubborn Cat will finally come around. They just require a little extra patience, but once they become potty-trained, it sticks.

🐾 🐾 🐾 🐾

The Tail Raiser

This somewhat rare trait can be found in spraying males, but it is also seen in some females. When urinating,

68

the "Tail Raiser" will start in a squatting position and raise their rumps (pushing hard and usually shaking the tail) until they are practically standing as they are going, thus sprinkling the whole back of the lid, or toilet tank if there is no lid. It turns into a real mess, and extremely hard to clean up, as the urine seeps into the seat hinges, underneath the tank and around the toilet bolts. It is a major clean up that you don't want to do regularly!

Hickory (at right) was one of the sweetest cats that anyone could ever hope for. However, she just could not break her habit of "rising to the occasion" when it came to going "#1". She trained well, being down somewhat in the toilet trainer, and did great with "#2". The hopes of her continuing to use the potty ended on Graduation Day, as she raised her rump and sprayed urine all over the toilet lid.

The Tail Raiser must be disqualified, since it's an inborn trait that can't be helped. It makes no difference how close you are with the cat. If you observe your kitty regularly raising their rump to be in a standing position as they go in the litter box, don't even go through the stress of training. Keep them happily using a covered, leak-proof litter box.

The Top Cat

The "Top Cat" is the leader of a multi-cat household, and comes in two different forms– the healthy and "Well-Adjusted" Top Cat, or the mentally unstable "Bully" Top Cat. They are polar opposites in the potty training realm.

The Well-Adjusted Top Cat doesn't have the need to bully anyone, and the other cats accept him or her as their natural leader. (Tovah was one at left.) These Top Cats are perfectly trainable, adapting well to the potty, and even help to train the other cats in the household. They are natural-born leaders that strive for the betterment of all felines. They see other cats as family, not of adversaries. They can be Close, Confident, Affectionate, Intelligent, any number of different traits, and excellent for potty training.

The unstable Top Cat is similar to the Arrogant Cat, and may not be a good candidate for training at all. They like things *their* way, and compromise is simply not in their vocabulary. They have to feel like they are always the one in charge, be it over feline or human. They usually prove to be more of a problem in a multi-cat household that is in potty training. In general, they may directly target one or more other cats and beat up on them, chase them incessantly, or steal their food or sleeping spot. They can eventually rebel and eliminate where they shouldn't. In a case like this, the other cats may be so stressed out by the Top Cat, that they might not feel comfortable enough to be potty-trained anyway.

An unstable Top Cat is much better as an *only cat* and most likely better suited for a litter box. Such was the case with Temima (above). Tovah and Temima were rivals.

🐾 🐾 🐾 🐾

The Water Hater

PHASES 1-3 are not much of a problem for the "Water Hater". However, when you get to PHASE 4, the cat may be afraid of the water and be terrified that they will fall in! This will often stress the cat out and they may refuse to go.

For the Water Hater, I highly recommend having a Travel Kiddie Potty Seat, which makes the hole smaller, and hides the water a bit more. I recommend putting it on during PHASE 3, as it makes the water less noticeable, and

71

it seems farther away. This way, they won't fear the water beneath them because they don't really see it as well. They will still hear a trickle as they go, but it won't be nearly as threatening to them. If the Water Hater is still scared, the next time they have to go, take off the kiddie seat, let them see down in the bowl, then put it on again so they can go using the seat. This repetition helps get them used to the idea, and then it isn't so scary after a while. Eventually it can be removed altogether. It works so well that it actually can build their confidence, and may even conquer their fear of the water! That is just what happened with Frankie as I finished up this book.

🐾 🐾 🐾 🐾

The Water Lover

PHASES 1-3 are no big deal for the Water Lover, but PHASE 4 is rough for the Pet Parent! Since the Water Lover doesn't care about getting wet, they may even end up playing in the toilet bowl. Some like to splash around in the water as though it were litter. This is obviously not ideal, especially if they like to sit down in the water, and decide to eliminate while they are *in the bowl*!

It is not impossible to train them though, they don't mind the potty at all. In fact, it is the next best thing to the litter box. For the Water Lover, it helps immensely to have a Travel Kiddie Potty Seat, which makes the hole smaller to keep the cat from going down into the water. Even this may not deter them from initially playing in the clean water. However, they will be forced to stay up on the seat away from the water. When they are done with their deposit, make sure to get their attention, praise them and give them their treat ASAP *away from the toilet*. This will keep them from wanting to go into the water and bury it. (Some may just become a bit of a Sloppy Cat if they don't mind washing their paws off.) After they have had their treat you can show them what they did while holding them, and flush it down immediately. The main thing with a Water Lover is to keep them away from the water if they try to play in it, and distract them if they try to go in it. Even though this goes against the general principle of "no distractions", Water Lovers become too fond of playing in the water and need some distraction to keep their mind on what they are doing!

The Young Cat

Young Cats are perfect for potty training, but younger Kittens really should not be trained until they are at least 3-4 months old, simply because they aren't very big yet. They can be aided with a Travel Kiddie Potty Seat, which makes the hole smaller for them to go on. The Young Cat does benefit from early training though. Going potty on the toilet becomes so ingrained in them, and becomes such a habit that when they are older, they will choose going on a toilet over the litter box if given a choice. They easily transfer to different toilets if moving or staying at a motel.

In looking at statistics, the younger a cat was when they came to me, the better they did with potty training. It likely has to do with imprinting on the Pet Parent and developing a closer relationship. The youngest cat who ever came to me was Loea (above), at about 4-weeks old. She started potty training at around 3 months old, and aside from a few relocation detours, went on the toilet steadily until age 18. That was really all she knew, and she was quite happy with it.

74

Chapter 5

Tips for Smooth Training and Transition

Keys to Success

This chapter is good sound advice from experience. Follow these tips to help make your transition smooth and successful.

🐾 🐾 🐾 🐾

Keep Your Cat Well Hydrated!

This is extremely important, because when a cat gets stressed, they can potentially get diarrhea, and are even more susceptible to dehydration. This can lead to serious health issues. During training, make sure there is always plenty of fresh clean water available at all times. A gravity waterer is a good investment, it doesn't run out very quickly. Just be sure to clean it at least every 1-2 weeks. (Even more often if the cat likes to put its toys in the water bowl!)

Making sure the cat is well-hydrated also forces them to have to go sooner. What goes in, must come out. It also helps the stools pass much easier, and indeed, when they are nervous, stressed and balancing the first few times, it is hard for them!

I like to add some extra water to the cat's food to make a "stew", which also helps get more water in them. You can easily check your cat for dehydration. Take the cat's skin near the scruff of the neck. Gently pinch and pull up on it, then quickly let go. If the skin springs back to place immediately, the cat is fine. If the skin stays bunched up and doesn't spring back immediately, the cat is dehydrated.

🐾 🐾 🐾 🐾

Make Sure They Like Their Treat

The "Potty Treat" or reward-giving ritual is a very important part of the process. If the cat isn't wild about their treat, they won't have any drive to get it. Very picky cats may have to have special treats to give them incentive. Perhaps a bit of tuna juice, or a bit of cooked meat. If a cat is not so driven by appetite, they may be the type to prefer extra interactive play or extra cuddling. It all depends on the cat's personality.

🐾 🐾 🐾 🐾

Don't Use Air Fresheners

Not only are the chemicals in air fresheners very bad for the cat (if not toxic), but it can ruin their sense of smell. They rely on scents as part of the training process. Cats have a very keen sense of smell, maybe not quite as much as dogs, but certainly far better than humans.

Air fresheners, and scented cat litter can be confusing to the cat, and the less confusion during this training time the better.

Don't Use Clumping Litter

Ideally, the best litter is good old fashioned clay granules, or even better, flushable litter is great for PHASES 2 and 3. As long as it isn't very much at a time, a tiny bit of flushed litter shouldn't be an issue. After all, a toilet was designed to take away human waste at a much larger volume than a small amount of litter. If your plumbing can't take it, there is something wrong with your plumbing!

Clumping litter has many drawbacks. First, it usually contains silica or harmful chemicals to make it instantly clump, which can be harmful to the cat's health. The company wants cleaning the litter box to be convenient for the human, not necessarily good for the cat! Next is the issue of plumbing. Indeed, because the clumps can get fairly large and are not designed to come apart easily, many people's plumbing really can't take it. The third issue is that some trainer pans have holes that the liquids go through to make for the "trickle" sound as the cat goes. Clumping litter would interfere with these and clog the holes, ending up making a big mess.

🐾 🐾 🐾 🐾

Proper Meals for All Cats

Please, please make sure your cat or cats have a good balanced diet, plenty of fresh water, and medical care when needed. Your cat's life depends on it!

A multi-cat household can be challenging in the area of feeding time. This is especially problematic when there are differing appetites. Ideally, all cats should be eating at the same time or same rate. If you have this, you've got it made!

Some cats are picky eaters that turn their nose up at most anything. Eventually they do have to eat. Find a good premium-quality diet to meet all of their nutritional needs, yet be attractive enough to the picky eater to make them want to eat the food.

A good majority of cats are nibblers, eating many small snack-like meals throughout the day. This is actually ideal for most cats, and some wet food can be used to supplement a bowl of dry food left for snacking at all times.

Then, there are those few kitties who are more like dogs in the respect that they will eat almost anything, and/or won't stop eating! They may have psychological issues, fearing that if they don't eat all the food they can at one sitting, it will be stolen from them and then they will starve. These types were usually crowded out by other kittens, or in a shelter where competition for food was high. The old gorging habit dies hard, even in the most loving of homes with little competition, they still tend to gorge themselves until they literally can become sick. Gorging can cause them to eat too much, can irritate their intestinal tract and cause bad diarrhea, sometimes with blood. They may gain or lose weight. If the problem persists, check it out with your vet, since it could indicate a health issue.

🐾 🐾 🐾 🐾

Proper Elimination

Healthy elimination is so very important, especially when it comes to properly potty training cats. It is nothing to mess with. I had a lovely kitty who died of constipation. It was a very rural area and the vet only visited town once every two weeks. By the time he had gotten her medicine to us it was too late, the toxins had built up in her system and affected her brain.

A healthy cat will be much more trainable. Make sure that any problems concerning eliminations are taken care of before starting potty training. These are not "fun" topics, but it's essential that your cat is doing okay in these areas. In multi-cat households, identification and knowing what the individual cat's stools (size, consistency, color, gaseous odor) and urine (volume, color) look like, can be very important if problems arise.

🐾 **#1:** Urination is vital, and should be a very light yellow. Cats may go on average 2-6 times a day, depending on the cat and its water intake. If a cat starts to go less often, especially if it is a male, it can be bad news. They should never be visibly straining. A newly- in-potty-training-cat may wait up to 24-36 hours the first time. If they wait longer than

36 hours, if there is blood in the urine, or they repeatedly try to go and nothing comes out, rush them to the vet immediately! Crystals and blockage are life or death situations.

🐾 **#2:** A healthy stool is firm and moist, comes out easily, and doesn't disintegrate upon contact with water. It shouldn't be rock hard or dry, nor should the consistency be like pudding or "soft serve ice cream". A normal adult cat generally goes 1-2 times a day, but can even skip one day without issue. If a cat goes more than twice, it may be overeating!

A cat should go nicely with only minor pushing. If they appear to be straining, or have blood or mucus, it may be problematic. Constipation or diarrhea can make it so hard for a kitty to train properly, and both can be exacerbated by stress.

Hard or dry stools may prevent the kitty from wanting to go on the toilet because it is painful for them, and can totally wreck the potty training. This can often be caused by dehydration.

At the other extreme, cats with loose stools or diarrhea may feel uncomfortable and have gas pains, so it too can be detrimental for training. Sometimes it can be caused by food allergies, and be accompanied by blood and excess mucus. Plus, when they go it can be loose and drip off of them as they rush and leave the potty area to get their coveted treat.

The wonderful thing about Potty Training is that Pet Parents can easily monitor their cats' urine output and stool consistency. If you ever need a sample for the vet, simply stick a disposable container under the cat as they go to catch a sample, and bring it to the vet. There will be no contamination of litter and little if any mess.

🐾 🐾 🐾 🐾

Sharing a Single Bathroom

If you have only one bathroom, you will most likely experience "Traffic Jams" now and then. Either multiple cats want to use the toilet at the same time, multiple humans, or both cats and humans want to go. It can be a challenge.

If two cats have to go, a regular toilet can fit both, but be sure they are lined up. They may need your help, or they could potentially go on each other's tails. (Been there done that!)

An alternate idea is to buy a portable potty for adults. There are plenty available online for campers and survivalists.

Making Kitty Comfy, and You Too!

It is essential to make your cat as comfortable as possible, so they relax and train well. But you don't want to be going crazy every time *you* have to use the toilet! Here are some tips that can make it a more comfortable experience for everyone.

- 🐾 *Only One Toilet***:** When you use the toilet, close the door. During the training process, which can last a month or more, the trainer box insert must be removed from the toilet and set somewhere as you go. Only allow cats to see it on the potty.

- 🐾 *For the Water Lover or Hater:* A Travel Kiddie Potty Seat keeps all cats out of the water, and is easily removed for you.

- 🐾 *For the Elderly or Younger Cat:* Place a small step stool next to the toilet to make the jump less high.

- 🐾 *For the "Furry-Footed":* Some options are to make a "Double Cat Toilet Seat", get a Travel Kiddie Potty Seat with a flat matte finish, apply adhesive non-skid tape to your seat,

 or trim your cat's paw fur with a moustache scissors (only if they don't squirm or it can be dangerous). All these ideas can help keep cats from falling into the water below.

FROM 1983-1993 (Left to Right)
SWEET P., ARTHUR, REGGIE & RODDY
JUNIOR, TOBY, HICKORY (w/ babies above),
PURRICANE & BLACKIE,
and LOEA (on my back).

KITTENGARDEN POTTY TRAINING
WELCOME TO THE THE CLASS OF 2020
KATERINA (Top)
FRANKIE (Bottom).

Chapter 6

Basic Training

Get with the Program!

After the bathroom/toilet area is readied, this is ultimately how the training will go. There are essentially 4 main phases, some more involved than others.

PHASE 1: Litter Box Location

Depending on the applicable situation, this may consist of one or two parts.

Part 1: For Resident Cats: The litter box must be relocated to the bathroom, if it isn't there already. Although seemingly ideal for cleanup, it should *NOT* be placed in the bathtub. (That already has given the cat the message that "this area is okay to go in".) If you have a half bath without a tub, it may be small, but the litter pan can be fairly small, just large enough to accommodate the cat comfortably. If only temporary, it can even be a simple aluminum roasting pan. If it is handy, it can be helpful to initially put a small sample of used litter or fecal matter in, just to get the scent in there, but this isn't absolutely positively necessary. It is only for the first-time use.

The litter box should be put into the bathroom for at least a week prior to training so that the cat knows that this is the place to go. (The old location should be cleaned thoroughly so that there are no leftover smells. Use "Odor Mute™" if there are any porous surfaces like tile grout, carpet or wood.) Cats are creatures of habit, and don't like major changes, so they must get accustomed to the new location. Once the cat is used to the litter box being in the bathroom, Part 2 of PHASE 1 can occur.

Part 1: For New Arrivals: Since the cat is unfamiliar with its surroundings, a new location for the litter box is not at all an issue! Newcomers can skip Part 1 entirely, and go straight to the trainer pan "Raised Litter Box" being put in place on the toilet (Part 2). Just to note, there are several styles of trainers available, and you can even make some yourself. (See Appendix for D.I.Y. Projects on page 171.)

Part 2: For Everyone: The trainer tray is placed on the toilet and filled with litter, so that it is now a "raised litter box". Simply show the cat the raised litter box. Set them on the toilet seat and let them sniff around and scratch a bit in the litter. Again, a little used litter or a small stool sample can be placed in it initially, just so it gets a little scent and they get the message that this is indeed a litter box and a safe place to go. Cats will often go in the dirt of raised flower beds, so this is not a huge stretch for them! Cats are not stupid, and understand that the litter is where they are supposed to go. There is a myth that cats must have their litter box slowly raised to the same height as the toilet in order to transition. This is totally untrue! Of all my many cats over 30+ years, I have never, *ever* had a problem with any cats getting confused by a "Raised Litter Box". They have an instinct for scratching, and covering up their business to discourage predators, and that is a much harder instinctual desire to overcome. Most of the time they will still scratch at the toilet or seat. Allow them to do it! It doesn't hurt anything and helps them remain well-adjusted.

Clean out the litter box or litter trainer tray after every single use with the cat watching, after having been given their special "Potty Treat" and lots of praise and petting. Start giving the cat a Potty Treat every single time they successfully go. This instills confidence and they relax more knowing that they are going where they should be and won't get in trouble.

One has to think like a cat, not a human. Some people think that PHASE 1 is a very difficult thing for the cat, when in reality, this is by far the easiest part. For both younger and older cats, a small step stool can be put in between the toilet and tub or wall to make the jump less high and the "Raised Litter Box" more accessible. I regularly use a stool next to the toilet. It simply helps make it easier for them. Some cats bypass the stool and just jump right up on the seat, but most seem to like it even if they don't really need it. Finally, pick the cat up and show them where to go. They will usually scratch around in there at first, giving it their "seal of approval". As the cat gets used to being "up", make sure to clean the litter box trainer well. You want to get the "box" as clean as possible, because cats will not want to go in a smelly area. You want just enough scent to attract them, but not enough to repel them. There is bound to be a tiny bit of used litter that falls aside into the clean, and that is just enough to have a hint that the cat can smell and you can't. They have an excellent sense of smell.

Important Notes: Whether having a litter box or a toilet trainer, one thing is fairly common for most new cats, *especially if they are young and nervous*. For the first 24-36 hours, the cat might not even go to the bathroom at all! At any more than 36 hours, this can start to get dangerous. (See "What If They Just Won't Go" on page 97.)

Remember, there is absolutely no set time for a cat to go through training. My best student (a new cat) skipped Part 1 of PHASE 1 entirely, to go on an instantly raised litter box, and completely graduated in 27 days without a single accident. (Not usually the norm!) My longest spanning student (can't say my "worst" student), trained fairly well, but due to her longer time spans in between going to the potty, it took her about 4 months!

PHASE 2: The Litter Lessens

This phase is fairly easy as well. Add new litter to the trainer litter box as needed. After a few days go by, as long as the cat is going both ways regularly, you can gradually decrease the amount of litter. This should go on for a few more days, until there is no more litter and the cat is scratching either on the seat or inside the trainer. Some trainer designs may be sieve-like, with holes allowing the urine to go through and make the trickling noise that they should get used to.

Be sure to give praise and a treat every single time they have gone on the toilet or trainer. (Yes, I am "like a broken record". I just can't stress the importance enough.) If they have happened to go without you being there, give them *even more* attention and treats. They earned it! That is an excellent indication that they are comfortable with going on the potty. They will remember, and know exactly what they did. Always be consistent!

🐾 🐾 🐾 🐾

PHASE 3: Water Starts to Appear

It starts to get a little harder as they progress through PHASE 3. Now, the trainer will start to have a little hole in the middle. Some trainers may still have a bit of litter in them, depending on their construction and instructions. For cats that are having a hard time adjusting to the hole, a little litter can be a good thing.

On a side note, I have found a very useful item that has helped immensely in potty training- a foldable Travel Kiddie Potty Seat that fits over the normal seat. This is great for younger or smaller cats, so that they don't accidentally fall down in to the toilet. Falling in the water at this stage could potentially spook the cat and ruin everything. The kiddie seat also helps those cats who fear water. Since the objective is to make the cat feel comfortable, it gets used to the seat and eventually may not even need it anymore. The kiddie seat also helps prevent the "Water Lover" cats from going down in the toilet to scratch in the water.

Throughout PHASE 3, the hole gradually gets bigger and bigger, exposing more water below. The cat should get used to each change gradually. Once they have gone on it several times, and they are visibly comfortable with it, they can progress to the next stage of the trainer's hole getting larger. This can go on over a couple of weeks or longer, depending on the cat, and they should not be rushed. Rushing can cause stress, and stress can cause health problems. It is essential that they feel relaxed and comfortable. Week by week, or few days by few days (depending on how many times they have gone ("Quantity"), make the hole in the center gradually bigger. Once this is achieved, they go to the next phase.

PHASE 4: Litter-Free and Loving It!

Graduation time! The trainer's hole has gotten so large that there is more water exposed than the trainer itself. All litter has been completely removed, and the cat should be scratching on the seat or the back of the toilet. (Water Lovers may scratch at the water.) Most trainers are completely removed at this point, and the cat should ideally be going on the toilet by themselves. By all means (and *even more so* now), keep giving the cat its treats and attention every single time they go. Ideally, it should continue every time they go, but eventually (and gradually) treats can be stopped. Really though, it's a bonding experience, and should be cherished, not viewed as an inconvenience. I wouldn't think of stopping the treats until at least after a year has gone by and they have had no "intentional" accidents. (By "intentional", I mean those that may go #2 on the floor rather than expending the effort to get up on the toilet to go.) Unintentional accidents, a "sticker" #2 that clings to a longhair's britches, or someone had a drip from diarrhea, cannot be helped, and never, *ever* blame a cat for something that it can't help.

Even well after they have "graduated", they will always relate the human toilet with their place to go. If you take them with you on a vacation in a motel room, or move to a new home, they will still view any toilet as being "their potty". Psychologically, the toilet has totally taken the place of a litter box. This will last the lifetime of the cat.

How Long Should It Take?

There is no set time for potty training. I have read ads promising things like, "Toilet train your cat in 3 weeks", etc. Don't believe it! Every cat is unique, and has their own time schedule. What works for one won't always work for another. The basic training method is the same, but that is about as far as it goes. It can be an easy process for some, but not all. The main thing to concentrate on is the comfort and stress level of the cat. When you approach training from this point of view, you will do well.

When the cat is to the point in its stage of learning that it does what it is supposed to on its own a few times, it can move to the next phase. Unless it is a multi-cat household, the cat should not stay in the same phase for too long. It can be hard to progress to the next phase since cats are creatures of habit and they get too used to it. Once they reach that historic final point of going on the toilet alone, give them more extra praise and attention.

Chapter 7
When Problems Arise
How to Handle It

Notice that the title of this chapter is "*When* Problems Arise", not "*If* Problems Arise". Life is almost never simple, but it is made easier if you know how to deal with problems before they *do* arise.

If you are familiar and prepared for what could happen, it isn't as stressful. As I always say, "Prepare for the worst, and the worst won't happen." Some little issues inevitably come up, so mental preparation is just as important as physical preparation.

🐾 🐾 🐾 🐾
"Stickers"

Some cats may have "stickers" or "cling-ons"- dry sticking stool, mucus, or other remnants that get stuck to the fur as they finish going. This is very typical for the very first time, and is never a concern for potty training. It can even happen to cats that use a regular litter box, most often to longer-haired cats. Sometimes the stool can be a bit dry and stick to the fur, or if the cat's stool is loose, it may just not have had enough force to get into the toilet or trainer pan and dribbles a bit onto their "britches". Despite the little bit of mess, first give a treat and praise for the cat going in the right place, and as they eat their treat, quickly try to clean up the residue. If it dropped on the floor, a disinfectant wipe can be used. If it remains on the cat, (after the treat) try using a piece of toilet paper or an organic baby wipe, pinching the area with the wipe and scraping the residue off of the fur between your fingers with the wipe. Hopefully the cat can clean the rest before they sit down on a non-cleanable surface like a cloth sofa or the like.

🐾 🐾 🐾 🐾

Starting to Go in the Wrong Place

If they haven't gone yet, but are just about started going where they shouldn't, it is okay to move a cat. Just be gentle, and do not jerk them up quickly as to punish them. You could potentially injure them. Simply pick them up from under their arms on either side, or you can even steady their backside cupping the outer part of their tail to support them with your other hand. Gently and carefully place them on the seat. They will naturally get their footing, and once they do you can let go. Once they are in the act, they are somewhat helpless, and have to complete their task. It is far more common that they try to poop on the floor than to urinate.

What to Do If It's Done In the Wrong Place

If you catch the cat "after the fact", you merely want the cat to feel guilty about their misdeed. Never, *ever* scream at the cat, hit the cat, or do anything that would "terrorize" it! This would only make the cat afraid. Then, instead of correcting the behavior, they may potentially go in a hidden place the next time.

If a cat urinates in the wrong place, it is not a very good sign at all. Make sure to clean it up as best as possible. I strongly suggest the use of an old enzyme product called "Odor Mute™". It is known to even kill skunk odor. Cats have excellent sense of smell. If they smell the urine in that place, they are highly likely to go there again. Keep the cat under very close observation. You may even want to keep them in the bathroom until they start to get the idea of where to go.

If a cat goes "#2" it is not quite as crucial. Sometimes, it can merely be due to an extra hard stool or gas pains, and it can just be painful. It is not great, but it can be just a real accident. In most cases, the cat will already feel bad for going where it shouldn't, and this is the objective. Calmly pick the cat up, take him to the

pile, set him down in front of it, and put its nose near the pile to smell it. You only want to get the point across that this is not good, and they will get this treatment every single time if they do not cooperate. In a calm and low voice, you should say something like, "Shame on you. You don't go there. Bad kitty!" With the cat watching and rubber gloves or toilet paper, pick up the "#2" and plop it into the litter trainer or toilet. As you do this, say (in as cheery of a voice as you can), "See, this is where you go! Good kitties go in the potty!" You may even want to add, "Good kitties who go in the potty get treats." Try to supervise the cat as much as you can, and if they *do* try to go in the wrong place again, pick them up while they are in the act (support their bottom and tuck their tail down to keep anything contained if you have to walk with them), and place them on the toilet seat. After they have gone, shower them with treats and attention.

If they repeat going next to the toilet on the floor in the bathroom, this behavior has to be "nipped in the bud". Do as above, putting the cat's nose near the little pile, and say in a low tone, "Did you do that? Did you do that? Bad [girl/boy/name]! You don't do that. Shame! No treat for you! Bad babies don't get treats." (I even go so far as to give them a feline growling sound, very soft, not loud. You don't want to freak them out.) Then, give them the silent treatment and don't pay any attention to them. Keep this up for a few hours if needed. It really bothers most cats, and they want to get back in your good graces.

Usually, the next time they will go "#2" in the toilet.

If this happens in a multi-cat household and you don't know who was the culprit, you can say, "Who did this?!" Usually, the guilty party will cower a bit more than the others or run, and the innocent ones may look a little worried but still look you in the eye. (If you can't tell who it was by the size or consistency of the deposit, or from the behavior of the cats, all can endure getting the nose put near the bad smell.) Finally, with the guilty cat watching, do as I said before, and say in a happy voice, "See, here's where you go!" Good kitties go here!"

🐾 🐾 🐾 🐾

What to Do If They Just Won't Go

Some cats can be very stubborn and refuse to go until they are practically bursting, and bloated from being so full, or gassy. Others are very loyal and don't want to do anything wrong, so they hold it since they think that they aren't supposed to go anywhere other than the litter box. These latter ones are the most dangerous. They are the type of cat that doesn't complain about anything. Just keep reassuring them that it is okay, they are not doing anything wrong. Hopefully they will finally go, and when that happens make a big fuss about it when they do. It is a great accomplishment for them! If they still just won't let themselves relax and go, they may have to be taken to the vet for a health check.

Travelling with Your Cat

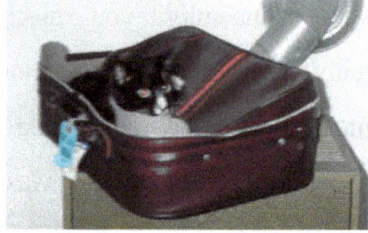

Much the same as for moving, potty-trained cats in your motel room are a piece of cake. The cats readily adapt to the new toilet just like any other one. If it is an elongated shape and you are afraid a smaller cat may fall in, you can always bring a portable Travel Kiddie Potty Seat. From my experience, even for small cats, it hasn't been an issue.

🐾 🐾 🐾 🐾

Moving

If you are in the process of moving and worry that your cat won't adjust or will lose their potty training, worry no more! This isn't such a big stretch for the toilet-trained cat. Simply show them where all the toilets are in the house. If you are moving relatively close by, it is no problem at all.

If you are moving farther away on a journey that is a few day's trip that can be a bit more problematic. If the cat has to fly in a plane, it can be somewhat traumatic being in the cargo hold. If they are brought aboard the plane with you, they are able to be comforted that they are with you, but they have to be so confined to such a tiny carrier that fits under your seat, that that they can barely move unless they are a small cat or kitten. They most likely will not go to the bathroom, unless they get too scared. If the trip is more than a day, perhaps the better option is to drive, and stay at motels. Then the cat can relax and actually continue to use the toilet unhampered.

It probably isn't the best idea to have your cat stop at a rest area or public restroom to go. They could break loose and get lost, some run blindly in a panic due to unfamiliar territory, or just plain get filthy dirty! In that event it would be better to temporarily go back to a litter box due to emergency circumstances. They can easily be retrained again.

🐾 🐾 🐾 🐾

Interruptions to the "Life of the Potty"

There are times when a cat may have to temporarily use a litter box through no fault of their own. It happens. During these times, it is important to remember that once they have been trained, they very easily can be re-trained back in about two weeks or so. It is already familiar to them, so it is somewhat "like riding a bike". The following are some examples as to certain events in life when a cat may have to "temporarily regress".

When Illness Strikes

Illness that causes a hospital stay can wreak temporary havoc with potty training. When a Pet Parent has to go in for a temporary hospital stay, one can usually find someone to just come in to feed the cat and flush the toilet. If the human has to stay for a good length of time, it is perhaps better for the cat to go stay with someone.

However, when the cat gets sick, it is usually a whole different scenario. The cat may be confined for a reason, like after a surgery, so that they move very little. In such a case, the vet is going to provide a simple litter box, and most likely not a toilet.

🐾 🐾 🐾 🐾

Boarding If Kitty Can't Travel

Sometimes boarding is an only option in events where you are: travelling someplace where the cat can't go; going to a place requiring a quarantine period; or travelling so many places that it's not practical to lug the poor cat around like a piece of baggage. Just as when a cat gets sick and has to stay at the vet's overnight or longer, most likely there won't be an available toilet for your cat. Whether boarded in a small cage or quarantined in a fairly large one, the cat will automatically use the litter box. Old habits die hard.

Not to worry though, they can be retrained even after a couple of years of using the litter box, because that behavior is familiar and (even if only subconsciously) "comfortable".

Another ideal option is to let the cat stay with a friend instead of a having a friend come over to take care of the cat now and then. I once had a 3-week trip abroad, and a cat-parent friend agreed to cat-sit in his home. He had his own cat with a nice litter box. I asked how it went when I returned to pick her up. He said he would have never known that there was another cat there, except for these few signs- he would occasionally hear hissing, her food would disappear, and there were little "presents left in the toilet overnight". This kitty preferred the toilet far more to the litter box (which was clean) even when given a choice.

🐾 🐾 🐾 🐾

Re-Training

This is when keeping your old trainer pan can really come in handy. You may need it for life's occasional unforeseen events. You'll need a small bag of litter, or maybe borrow some from a friend. Simply do the regular phases all in order. They will go to each next phase far quicker than when they were first being taught. At most it should probably take two weeks. It seems to be very much "like riding a bike" for the cat.

Old Age

When a cat gets older, some problems can arise. Arthritis can set in, making it painful to jump up and down from the floor to the seat, or it can be harder to balance. In this case, I highly recommend putting a small step stool next to the toilet. It makes it so much easier for the senior cat to go.

I would recommend making a Double Cat Toilet Seat with non-slip tape attached. It makes it much easier for a senior to hold onto the seat and balance. My seniors kept going on the toilet until nearly the ends of their lives, when they had become incontinent before their deaths (one of kidney failure in old age, and the other of a stroke a few years after a diagnosis of cardiomyopathy, respectively). They were either just too weak to make it up on the toilet, or couldn't hold it until they got there. (I do not have photos of them, since I prefer to remember them in their younger happier state. It was beneath their dignity to take pictures.)

Elderly incontinence can happen even if you have a litter box, so it really is not an issue of being potty-trained or not, it is more of a medical issue. The two seniors ended up having custom-made kitty diapers (dog diapers had the tail hole too high), and went about their remaining days/weeks in the diapers without complaint. They had really wanted to get up on the toilet, but knowing they could no longer make it, they peacefully accepted their conditions, never trying to take the diapers off. They seemed to know and understand what they were for.

Some tips on making custom cat diapers: Use infant diapers for most cats, and some masking tape for sealing the tail holes. (Duct tape is overkill, and it sticks too well, potentially grabbing on to your cat's fur and hurting them.)

Create a pattern "template" with the first one, you will need it for subsequent ones. Once you cut holes in the correct place in the diaper, beware that many diapers use tiny silica beads for liquid absorption. You want to keep these little potentially-toxic items contained. When you make the cut, seal it up immediately with pieces of masking tape all around the hole to connect the inner and outer sides and completely seal the hole so there are no gaps. You may have to experiment with fitting the diaper a few times before you get the tail hole in just the correct place and at just the correct width.

Masking tape works very well, since diapers are only temporary, and the absorbent medium keeps it dry enough that by the time any liquid would get to the tape you would be changing the diaper anyway. I never had any problems with leakage.

Multi-Cat Households

It is not at all impossible to teach a houseful of cats to use the toilet. I have never trained more than three cats at once, but it may be advisable to have more than one toilet if there are more cats than that. Be prepared for Traffic Jams, especially upon coming home from being out. Whether litter box trained or potty-trained, one thing I have noticed throughout my history of living with cats is that they tend to get very excited when you come home. Usually, this excitement leads to having to go.

While in the old days of litter, maybe 2 cats would be in each litter box at the same time, it isn't quite as easy for cats to share a toilet. However, it isn't impossible. Two smaller cats can comfortably sit together on a regular sized seat, and unless their tails are draped in the toilet, in the path of a crossing a stream or other "falling objects", they should be able to go together. If cats are larger, then they'll just have to go one at a time. You may have to be the judge as to who should go first if needed, and keep the others sidetracked.

New Cats and Quarantining

If a new cat is quarantined to the bathroom, don't feel guilty. If you boarded your cat at the vet, they would probably be sitting in a cage at least 5 times smaller. It is best to keep new cats "quarantined", and away from the already resident cats. They can play "footsie" with each other underneath the door, as they get used to each other's smells and sounds. It makes for a much smoother transition in general for everyone. Depending on the cat personalities involved, they usually take 2 weeks to totally get adjusted to each other. If both cats are friendly and like other cats (at least from the safe distance of looking out the window), they may take as little as 2 days.

During the quarantine period is an excellent time to start potty training a new addition. A new cat can start directly on Part 2 of PHASE 1, entirely skipping the "relocation of the litter box", to an immediately "raised litter box". At the point in which the new kitty is introduced the residents, they should be far enough along in training that it won't really hurt the others to go back a few steps. I have found this method to be extremely successfully, and the resident cats even help train the new cats.

FROM 1995-2020 (Left to Right)
SWEET P. & LOEA (watching TV), TOVAH,
TEMIMA, KATANA.
KATERINA, and FRANKIE.

Chapter 8
Meet the Cats!
Ten Real-Life Cat Case Examples

Originally back in 1989/90 when I first started potty training cats, I certainly had no intention of writing a book on it, and didn't document it step by step in pictures. Fortunately, even with all the moving I have done, some pictures still survived.

Meet ten of the cats that helped to form the basis of this book. Although these are just *some* of the cats I have had over my lifetime so far, they are an extremely diverse group. They vary greatly in temperament, personality, intelligence, and physical characteristics. Boys, girls, kittens, "teenagers", mothers, elders, longhairs, shorthairs, purebred, and humble alley cats. How did they all come to me? Travel the unique journeys of each of their lives, and experience their "adventures" in potty training. They are listed in the order of the dates when they learned.

The majority are rescues, most coming to me at a fairly young age. I will provide as many pictures as I can, but between moves and lack of having a camera, some are only "documented" in my memories. Nonetheless, I hope to share some nice kitty stories with photos, and what cat-lover can resist that! Enjoy my special fur baby stories...

1. Sweet P. – The Close Cat

Birthdate and Departure: I estimated Sweet P.'s birthdate at March 20, 1983, and always kept it as that date, as I did for all of my kittens when they arrived. (For those adopted older, sometimes their date of arrival was kept as their official day.)

In 2003, after having her last bout with kidney failure, and needing subcutaneous hydration, she had been put in diapers. (See her Potty History later.) I had been tending to her all day, and finally had eaten a bit of frozen pizza for dinner. I looked at the clock next to me which had just turned midnight. I looked down at Sweet P. who was laying in my arms and I said, "Oh look Sweet P., it's your 21st birthday! Happy Birthday! She slightly raised her head, kneaded in the air 3 times, and just quietly slipped away.

How Sweet P. Arrived: When I was 19-years-old, I sold hand-painted T-shirts on consignment for a dog grooming place down the road that also sold pet items and gifts. One particular day when I went there, to my delight they had a glass case at the register full of beautiful and lively 8-week-old kittens, that "someone had found in the wild".

I was looking at all of these adorable babies, and there must have been about seven. There were a lot of solid Russian Blue-looking types, and the others were bi-colors, mostly in blue and white, with symmetrical markings. They all played together and were totally oblivious to me. All except for one particular little kitten, who stationed herself directly in front of me, on the other side of the glass. She was doing absolutely everything she possibly could to get my attention, like turning summersaults and rolling around, always looking directly at me. Who could resist this rather comical looking kitten with black on one cheek and swirls of white streaks here and there?! Sweet P. eventually turned out to look like a beautiful Norwegian Forest Cat, complete with the double coat. She also had unique brown flecks in her pretty green eyes.

Assessed Traits: A shining example of the Close Cat, she was also Affectionate, Disciplined, Fastidious, Furry-Footed, Good, and Older (having been both the oldest to start training, and the longest-lived).

Life with Sweet P.: I had pre-planned to get a kitten, and had a name all picked out if they were gray or silver - "Quicksilver".

That name never took, she just wasn't a "Quicksilver", she was my little "Sweet P.". She was in every essence my "baby". We were pretty much inseparable, wherever I was, she was sure to be found. We would sleep together, usually she would be in the crook of my left arm, but if I weren't around, or if she decided to move, she would sleep on my pillow, (which is her whole name "Sweet Pillow Cat"). She would often wash my face. As with other cats, "mutual grooming" is a great honor, or so I took it as such. I obviously couldn't reciprocate in the same exact way, but instead would use my chin to stroke the top of her head as though I were washing her with my tongue. She always liked that.

We did everything together. If I was in another room and she lost sight of me, she would go around the house calling out, "Mowma... Mowma?!" until she found me.

Sweet P. was a master at playing hide and seek. Sometimes we were both into it so intensely that we got injuries running after each other. Peer around the corner, go back, peer around the corner, here she comes. Run! Next turn, go hide. She comes to find me, and when I see her chase! She at one point slid into a cabinet knocking out a tooth, and I at one point slid on a rug and fell flat on my face. We were a bit more careful after that.

Other games involved playing "stringy", where a piece of rope or twine would be dragged across the floor and she would chase it, sometimes catching it and carrying it away. This was always done under supervision with a human on the other end of the string.

Potty History: Sweet P., along with Junior, were my first two cats to be potty-trained. Sweet P. was 6 years-old when she first learned, perhaps the oldest of all to learn at the time. After ordering a potty training kit from an ad in the back of an issue of *Cats* magazine, the cats were ready and willing. They both trained beautifully, and there were no issues or problems at all.

Her "Potty Ritual" was to jump up on the seat, walk around, jump down, repeating it many times, and meowing throughout. She did eventually do her business after that, and did not leave the scene like other cats have done. She just stayed jumping up and down and all around until she was ready and did it.

Sweet P. has earned the distinction of having gone on

more different toilets than any other cat – 12 different living locations in 4 different states. (It would actually be 14 different locations if you were to count temporary motel stays, but still, they are different toilets!)

I was newly married in a tiny efficiency apartment with only one toilet, so things could sometimes get a bit hairy. With two adult humans and two adult cats, potty "Traffic Jams" could occur. Fortunately, everyone's potty schedules were pretty different. That is not always the case.

Early on, when it was still new for the cats to use the potty, we were about to go on a trip. They could go in the potty for a couple of days and it shouldn't be much of an issue since neither cat tried to go down in the bowl or dig to cover it up. Plenty of food and water were left out. Earlier that day, there was a problem with the fan vent in the bathroom above the toilet. It was easily fixed, and we quickly rushed out the door to get to the airport. It had only been two days, but when we got back, we entered the apartment and nearly started to gag. We then remembered that when the fan was being fixed, the toilet had been used as a ladder. The only problem was, in the rush to leave, nobody remembered to put the toilet seat lid back up and the poor cats had no way to use the potty! They did the next best thing and used the bathroom sink instead. Very logical, as it was the same round shape and color as the toilet bowl.

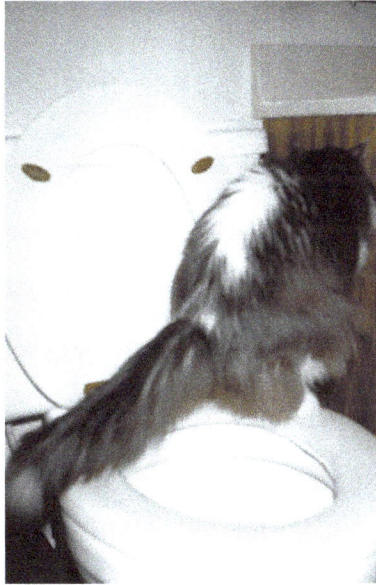

Throughout our lives together, there were many potty "interruptions" that were beyond our control, such as frequent relocation, one of which was she had a 4-month quarantine in Hawaii at 10 years old. (It is now only 3 months.) Sweet P. was a champion throughout it all. When we were reunited, she retrained quickly. Originally, she wasn't going to make the trip, but we realized that she might just pine to death from missing me. Indeed, during the quarantine period, she was deeply depressed and wouldn't respond at all to her caregivers at the quarantine facility. When I came to visit her, she perked up a bit and at least moved around. Finally release day came and she was back to her old cheerful self. She always relearned the potty without problem. For her, it was much like a human "riding a bike". Once she knew it, she only required a brief refresher course.

When she was 17, (above) Sweet P. suddenly had a little blood in her urine (never again after that), so we rushed her to the vet. They said she was old and to "get prepared to expect the worst". Her diagnosis was that she was starting to have kidney failure. She was also having a little trouble with arthritis, so we put a spare toolbox between the toilet and the bathtub to act as a stool. This helped her immensely. Later, as she was slipping a little on the seat (after all, she was "Furry-Footed" Cat), so I trimmed her paw hair, and we eventually made a Double Cat Toilet Seat with anti-skid tape. This worked perfectly, and she continued to use the potty flawlessly until a few days before her kidneys finally did give out at age 20. She tried relentlessly to get on the toilet but just couldn't make it, she was too weak. She had the most depressed and disgusted look on her face as she simply had to go "#1" on the tile floor next to the toilet. She would still try a few more times to get on the toilet, but we ended up making her some custom diapers. Sweet P. still contentedly slept in my arms every night until the very end. I still miss her even after 17 years.

Conclusion: If you have a close relationship with your cat like this, you will go very far in potty training. There is already that built-in mutual respect and love for each other there, and they have an automatic will to want to please you. Often, that is their sole motivation, the love for their Pet Parent, and longing to be close with them and please them.

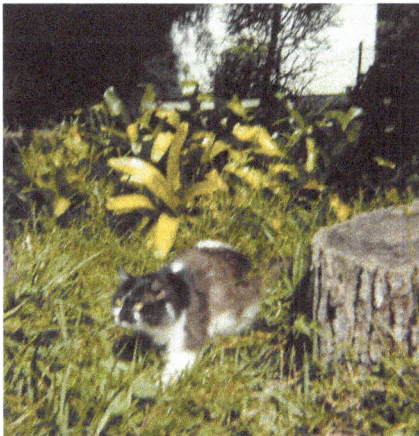

2. Junior - The Obedient Cat

Birthdate and Departure: Junior's birthday was on November 22, 1997. Everyone loved him – feline and human alike. He died at 13, from a tumor on his lung that was too close to the spine to operate. Everyone was crying that day – including my mother who we called from the vet's office to get her vote on making the tough, sad decision to let him go in peace. He will be always be remembered for his sweet nature.

How Junior Arrived: We planned to get another kitten, after our beloved Tumbleweed "Kitty" (my 3rd), had died. Junior's story was an odd one. My mother and I found a kitten in the classified ads listed "Free to a Good Home". We called the number, and they gave us their address to come and pick it up. We called a cab, and we drove around and around, but the address simply did not exist! We called the number back, and they said someone had come to get the kitten, so it was no longer available.

As fate would have it, I went to the same groomer's place where I got Sweet P. Pinned to their bulletin board was an ad for a kitten from one of their employees. It was all arranged, and Tumbleweed Jr. (known as "Junior") was delivered to us in a small box. The other cats (8 at the time) simply fell in love with him! Another kitten of two days less than 8-weeks old, he was a small "Tuxedo" kitty, shiny short black fur with white paws and chest, and cute little white moustache on his black cheeks.

Assessed Traits: A shining example of the Obedient Cat, he was also Affectionate, Fastidious, and Good.

Life with Junior: Junior was loyal and obedient to the max, always wanting to please. He would frequently act as though he thought he was doing something wrong, and would look at you with big sad and worried eyes. Once consoled, he would be back to purring and kneading.

Junior was such a good boy that he would obediently choose right from wrong. He could distinguish between two different surfaces. The white bar counter top on the living room side he was allowed to go on. Attached, directly behind on the same level was the black kitchen counter that he was not allowed to sit on. Amazingly, no matter if there was food or any other temptation, he would never set foot on that "forbidden" black counter. Always affectionate and purring, he was known for his curling his tail into a circle since kittenhood.

Although he was a real ham as a kitten, he became camera

shy later on, and I regret to say that I never got a single picture of him going on the potty. Perhaps it was the flash that scared him, but back in those pre-digital days, (unless you were a professional photographer), that was the only way to properly light a subject.

Junior would also play "stringy" in much the same way as Sweet P., and they would take turns.

Potty History: When he first trained with Sweet P., all went

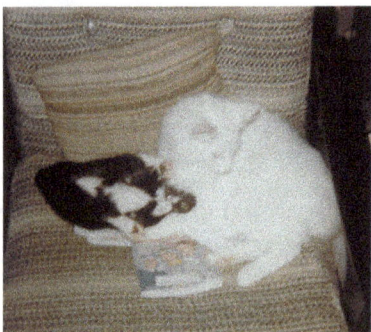

smoothly. Apparently, they gave each other silent moral support. Junior had the most endearing "Potty Ritual" habit of when he would get up on the seat to go, he would shuffle his little back feet side to side and back and forth for quite a while until he got just the perfect footing. He would always perch to go with his back toes curled over the edge.

When we moved locally, but still several minutes away by car on a cold winter night, it was rather chaotic. The 55-gallon aquarium was moved next to last, but the pair of large Tin-Foil Barbs went into shock in the 5-gallon bucket they were in, so they had to get priority. The cats were one of the last items to be moved, and after the apartment had been emptied out, and they were all alone in the dark for several hours until we could come get them, they were very freaked out. Not the norm, it wasn't the smoothest transition for Junior. Already being a little on the nervous/insecure side, Junior went beyond typical in that he held his first urine for almost 48 hours. This is especially not good for a male, and on that occasion, he was taken to the vet to relieve him by force. Junior was always so concerned that he would be going where he shouldn't, that he literally held it too long. This was very typical for him only with moving, and not the other cats. The strange thing is, that he did fine on trips where we stayed in motels for a short time. He would hop up on the potty and go!

Junior, like Sweet P. had many interruptions due to relocations and he had a gap in potty-ability due to staying in a different home. He sometimes was prone to cystitis, so it was thought to be better for him to stay behind where he could have instant access to an emergency vet if needed. His potty hiatus lasted 4 years (part of this time Sweet P. and I were in Hawaii), but when things finally got settled and he was able to be reunited with us, he relearned potty in only about two weeks. Having lost the original trainer pan over the years, and nothing remotely similar was available at the time, the potty trainer consisted of an old ceramic pot lid filled with litter, which fit perfectly into the toilet bowl. For a short time after another relocation, he almost developed the habit of going in the bathroom sink, (perhaps remembering the past mishap and going in the sink? - see Sweet P.'s story) but after the sink was covered so couldn't go there, he stopped and was fine after that. He resumed using the potty for 3 more years.

Conclusion: If you have an Obedient Cat, they are born for potty training! Chances of "accidents" (or "accidentally on purpose") are pretty slim. The kitty will most likely go on the potty their entire life without deviation, unless there's a health issue.

3. Hickory - The "Tail Raiser"

Birthdate and Departure: Her true birthdate was unknown, so we celebrated her adoption date of March 11, 1990.

Several years after she moved to my mother's, Hickory developed a voracious appetite yet was losing weight. She died around 2004-5 a few years after being diagnosed with Hyperthyroidism. She lived a very happy, quality life 14 years longer than if she stayed at the SPCA.

How Hickory Arrived: Hickory came to us at about 6-8 months old. Always friendly to everyone, with a pretty combination of "smoky" colors (hence the name "Hickory", like hickory smoke), greyish patches and brown tabby with semi-long hair. My husband at the time worked for a landlord, who sometimes bought houses to fix up and rent out. We were in charge of renovations on one particular property he had acquired, which was a very old house. Hickory had been one of many stray cats that the former occupant had been feeding before having been evicted. One day, Hickory got into the house and hid for several days in a hole in an attic closet that led to underneath the floorboards and the bathtub plumbing. There was a nice kitty-sized hollow area under the tub that was totally inaccessible by a human unless they were to rip out the heavy old porcelain enameled cast iron bathtub. One could only tell that a cat was residing in the house due to the food disappearing from the Have-a-Hart humane trap, and the occasional dry "potty gift" in the corner when nobody was there working at night. Every single day we would bait the trap with tuna and other cat food

goodies before we left for the day, and each time, she somehow would trip the trap and manage to not get caught. She outsmarted us nearly every time!

One day we got wise to how she might be just be skipping over the trip mechanism, and set a large tile spanning the length of trap's trip lever and where the tuna can would sit, so that when she was about to go out, her weight would shift the tile and trip the trap. Finally, that worked and we caught her! Our boss actually found her in the trap and left us a happy message on the answering machine, "... You can relax. The cat is in the cage, *the cat is in the cage*! ..."

We brought her to the local SPCA thinking she would find a home, but we had first dibs at adopting her. They contacted us and said, "The cat is going to be destroyed, do you want her?" Of course, we would take her, but why would such a beautiful cat be destroyed? It turned out she was pregnant! Hickory came to live with us and we all awaited the day of the kittens' arrival.

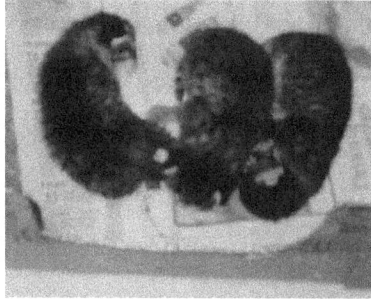

Assessed Traits: She exemplified the "Tail-Raiser". Her other traits included being Affectionate, Furry-Footed, and Good.

Life with Hickory: Hickory was a sweetheart from the get-go. She had the cutest habit of what I called "jump shots" – when you would go to pet her, she would "meet you half-way" by jumping up slightly on her hind legs to almost force you to pet her. She dearly loved to do "head butts', where she would bump her forehead against my forehead. Sometimes she did it very hard, but it was her own way of being affectionate. She was always affectionate and kneading, purring like a motor boat, and had somewhat of a scratchy voice when she meowed. When we brought her home from the SPCA after having a clean bill of health (except for her pregnancy), she was quite matted. I had a flea comb for combing out her beautiful coat, and aided with some scissors I started cutting out the mats. On one occasion I got a bit too close to the skin (which was the same color as her fur) and didn't know it, until afterwards when I saw some slight bleeding. I had grazed her skin in a small patch. I felt so terrible! Poor, Hickory never let out a peep or even flinched! After treating the wound, this time I continued cutting into the mats themselves, staying far away from her skin. It took extra time, but I was finally able to remove them all. What a patient and good kitty!

She got along wonderfully with the other cats after the initial two introductory weeks of growling from a slightly jealous Sweet P. After all, it was now three kitties (which would double) in our tiny one-room efficiency apartment. There was no way to do a quarantine situation there! After a few weeks, Hickory started getting very aggressive with Junior who literally wouldn't hurt a fly, but she would suddenly attack him for seemingly no reason. A few days

later, Hickory had her litter of three kittens right in the middle of the kitchen floor after having had a treat of a little macaroni and cheese.

Potty History: Prior to her kittens' birth, Hickory went into potty training, and ultimately so did the already trained Sweet P. and Junior. All went well, except for one thing– Hickory was apparently used to spraying in the wild, and raised her tail as she went! Rather unusual for a female, perhaps it was part of her survival methods. This made for a huge mess all over the back of the toilet seat and tank.

Although we thought going on a potty may force her to perch and hold her tail down, it just didn't happen. Her behavior was too ingrained. After just the one time, Hickory was relieved of potty privileges, and Sweet P. and Junior went back to using the potty like nothing had ever happened.

A special screen cover was made for the bathtub that sat on its ledges. Hickory and her kittens were kept there within the bathtub using a litter box for everyone's protection. She and the kittens were later taken in by my mother who already had several cats that used a covered litter box. It worked out for everyone.

Conclusion: If you have a "Tail Raiser", they are best suited to using a litter box. It's not that they *can't* be trained, Hickory was willing and sincerely tried. They just can't seem to change this behavior either because of a mental block, their muscles and build won't allow them to, or perhaps a combination of factors.

4. Arthur - The Arrogant Cat

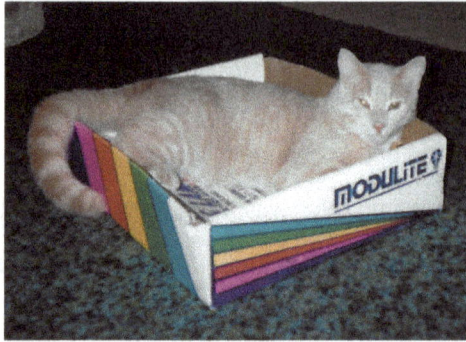

Birthdate and Departure: Arthur was a stray adopted on October 22, 1984. He later became a single cat on a farm, and lived happily ever after being his own Top Cat.

How Arthur Arrived: I pegged him at about 5-6 months old.

One day he came sauntering into our backyard in Florida like he owned the place. He was a very charming, handsome cream tabby, and since nobody posted any lost cat notices, my mother and I took him in.

Assessed Traits: His most blatant trait was being Arrogant. He also was Confident, Intelligent, Spiteful, Stubborn, and although he started out as a healthy Top Cat, he eventually became an unstable bully of a Top Cat.

Life with Arthur: Arthur was highly intelligent, he knew it, and was very arrogant. He had a very complex personality–

the charming villain, that you secretly routed for and just couldn't stay mad at. He taught himself to open cabinet doors and steal the dry cat food, scale the highest of doors, and look at you in the eye as he did something wrong. He wanted to do everything his own way, and would let you know if something displeased him.

To demonstrate the complexity of his personality, this sometimes relentless bully also had a surprisingly gentle and nurturing side, which added to his charm. On two different occasions, (several years apart) a pair of small kittens came to live with us, that had obviously been taken from their mothers too soon. Arthur would wash them and take care of them as though he were their mother, to the extent that he actually let them nurse on him!

Arthur would sometimes play soccer with toy balls, but he got more joy from chasing other cats.

Arthur was fearless, and didn't let anyone push him around. He would even challenge tough humans who didn't like cats by getting "in their face". Our cat-hating boss had a meeting with us one day at our apartment to discuss some things. Arthur was so arrogant, that he jumped on the counter, where the boss had his briefcase, and was sitting.

Arthur went right up to him to sniff at him and give him the stare down, so our boss gave him a hard flick on the nose in return. It didn't even faze Arthur. He just kept trying to pester our boss during the meeting until he had to leave.

Potty History: As the "tail-raising" mother Hickory (see previous story) was still nursing her babies, Arthur, (who was still living with my mother) would relentlessly terrorize and chase two of her other cats, TuffyNuff and Peanuts to the extent that they had to hide from him and they just couldn't move. Knowing how intelligent Arthur was, I thought he could learn to go on the potty. We swapped Hickory in exchange for Arthur, hoping it would give the other cats some peace. Being very intelligent, he did potty train quickly and well.

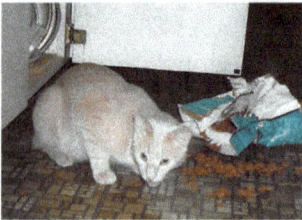

His "Potty Ritual" was a combination of actions, jump up, shuffle slightly while wiggling his bottom side to side, and just go all within a few seconds. He was so confident in all that he did, that he didn't make any fuss about it, or feel that he had to have a good footing. All was fine until one day he just decided he had enough of it. Apparently, the novelty or more likely the challenge, wore off. To show his

128

final opinion, he climbed into the most difficult, hard-to-get-to place, up and under some craft supply baskets in the closet. This could not have been comfortable! He decided to relieve himself all over my craft yarn. Knowing that yarn could mean potential death to a cat if ingested, it was kept completely out of reach and safely tucked away inside a plastic bag within the baskets so that no cats could ever get to it, that is except for Arthur. Once he started this, he refused to stop. He still would still use the potty, but decided to supplement on my yarn. He was promptly sent back to my mother who found a home for him through her veterinarian.

Conclusion: If a cat is Arrogant, it's bad news. Top Cats that feel they're superior to everyone else, human and feline alike, may be trainable, but it's likely not going to stick in a multi-cat household. They may be fine as an "only cat" where they can be their own boss. Potty train at your own risk!

5. Loea - The Intelligent Cat

Birthdate and Departure: Loea was born in a thicket of *lantana* on August 11, 1993.

In her later years she was diagnosed with cardiomyopathy, and later had a stroke. She lived to 18-years-old and ended up having custom kitty diapers when she was too weak to go on the potty. She was loved and admired to the very end.

How Loea Arrived: This is a fascinating, very detailed story, but worth the time to read. It really shows the lengths that cats will go to communicate something important.

In 1993, we had relocated to a rural area in Hawaii. As Sweet P. was doing her time in quarantine on Oahu, we were living and working on a sea farm that produced shrimp and various types of fish. There was a sea farm cat,

130

I called "Sea Breeze", a handsome and affectionate tom. Another cat resided in the area, a petite female feral cat who lived in the forest of *kiawe* and *koa* trees. I called her "Spot", which had a double meaning, since she was a spotted tabby, and she liked to hang around with the dogs. She ran when she saw any humans, but I befriended her bit by bit with my special treats of sun-dried minnows that were always present after a shrimp harvest. After a few weeks, Spot started looking very plump, and as I had suspected, she was pregnant. Her time to deliver came, and on that day, she disappeared for two days, then reappeared visibly thinner.

About one month passed, and Spot was not looking very good. She was visibly thin, and appeared to have a fever. She came up to me, meowed, and walked a short distance. She looked back at me, meowed and walked some more, obviously wanting me to follow her. She brought me to the midst of the forest, where there were large boulders situated amongst a thicket of lantana. She stopped there, meowed, and disappeared into the thicket as though to say, "Wait here". A few minutes passed, and she finally came out of the thicket. She looked back at the hole where she emerged and

131

meowed. Out stumbled a tiny kitten that looked just like her! The little 4-week-old kitten came right over, unafraid, and I was able to pet her, no problem. Spot meowed again, at the hole, then nothing happened. She approached closer to the hole and meowed at it again looking somewhat annoyed. Out popped another kitten that looked just like Sea Breeze! This little kitten took one look at me and hissed at me!

It seemed that Spot needed help with her first litter of kittens. It was visibly draining her, and she was getting sick from it. Every day I brought some prepared infant formula soy milk that one of the workers had on hand for her now-weaned baby. Spot completely disappeared after a few days. She obviously trusted me with her precious babies, and knew they were in good hands. Sadly, I thought she had gone off to die somewhere. I tended to the kittens as best as I could with the limited supplies available. I began adding fish and meat to the powdered soymilk, eventually getting some real kitten food at the store when they were old enough. The kittens were getting very rambunctious, starting to outgrow the kitten nest and roam a little farther. There was an owl starting to hang around the sea farm, and a kitten would likely make a nice snack for it. I made the decision to bring the kittens inside. I filled a pan with gravel that was used to level up the large fish tanks outside, and it was a perfect litter box, the gravel looked much like clay kitty litter, which of course, the kittens had never seen before. Kiko and Loea immediately took to it without needing any instruction. We were temporarily sharing our boss' home until we fixed up a shack on the premises. The little female kittens now occupied their guest bathroom. I made a litter box and they seemed quite happy. The spotted tabby who looked like mother Spot I named "Kiko", which is Hawaiian for "Spot". The one that looked like daddy Sea Breeze was highly intelligent and I called "Loea", which means "clever" or "smart" in Hawaiian.

As a happy note to the story, Spot reappeared at the back door on the deck when the kittens were about 8 weeks old, and she looked great! She apparently just needed to rest, and knew that she wasn't physically capable to support the nursing kittens and herself.

Assessed Traits: Obviously as named, she is Intelligent. She was also Confident, Disciplined, Fastidious, Good, eventually Sick, but also Young at the time of her learning potty.

Life with Loea: A dainty 5-lb. girl with an "H" on her back in white, she was one of the youngest cats to ever potty train, and certainly the smallest. Even as a kitten you could tell this tiny creature was different, observing every little thing, and teaching herself through what she saw. She figured out at about 8 weeks old that if she lifted up on the bathtub faucet's diverter valve with her teeth and dropped it, fresh water would drip out of the faucet. When she got older and could jump up on the vanity, she somehow figured out how to turn the doorknob next to it and open the door to get out. Loea was slightly less than 3 months old when Sweet P. had gotten out of quarantine and joined us. When Sweet P. came, the boss decided to take Kiko for his little son, and she exited the bathroom. After having had four long months of mandatory litter box in the quarantine, Sweet P. was ready to go back to the toilet. Sweet P. was 10 years older than Loea, but the two got along so well.

Although she wasn't terribly affectionate, Loea loved us all in very much an intellectual's way, and would never leave one's side if they were sick, whether it was Sweet P., or me. She would stay there near the patient making sure they were okay.

134

Loea was so creative, and used her paws like hands. It was quite funny when she would flip through the phone book as though she was looking

something up. One day I came back home and found she had done a search on my computer for "H", (it remains a mystery to this day as to how she did it). She taught herself how to play ping pong, without any coaxing from me at all. The game just spontaneously evolved. She would stand on the bed, I would bounce the ball to her, and she would bat it back, at times using alternating paws. These games went on for several minutes at a time, until one of us missed the ball or it got bounced out of range. Her exploits were so unique that I created her own little website so that I could share her ping pong and potty videos. Sadly, the technology advanced but was no longer compatible, and the videos are no longer very high quality. I did manage to get a few pictures from them.

She and Sweet P. enjoyed watching videos of birds, and even were caught watching some germs moving about in a documentary. Loea liked to open cabinet doors, drawers, and even managed to somehow turn doorknobs and open actual doors. Unlike Arthur, she didn't do it to steal food or get into trouble, she seemed to do it just for the challenge alone. Once she would achieve her goal, she would just walk away.

Loea like most geniuses, had some funny quirks, such as she would always test her drinking water with her paw before she drank, and liked to stand on the very top of her 2x4 carpet-covered scratching post, just balancing like that for a few minutes at a time. It seemed as if she was exercising for her "Potty Ritual".

Potty History: A plywood insert was crafted to fit between the seat and rim, and an old pool skimmer was stapled to the plywood. This turned out to be an excellent trainer! Training went smoothly and both Sweet P. and Loea were retrained/trained in about three weeks. Loea was a very fast learner, and not stubborn.

Her "Potty Rituals" involved jumping up on the seat, walking

around on complete time, getting into position, and perching with all feet close together as though she were standing on her scratching post and had no room. Sometimes she got down and repeated it. For going "#2", she would sit on the seat, and her front feet she would use to jump up and down, which seemed to help her with leverage to push it out. Often, she would go with one paw raised for a short time.

After returning to the Mainland, Loea and Sweet P. had to temporarily go off of potty while we were getting resettled. Of course, she took to it right away again with very little retraining. Eventually Junior rejoined us, also going back to the potty, and they peacefully

coexisted for the rest of Junior's life, which was relatively short in comparison. Loea continued to go potty flawlessly her whole life until after her stroke, preferring the potty to any litter box. This was demonstrated when she was staying with a friend of ours who had a cat while we were on vacation abroad for 3 weeks.

Conclusion: Intelligent Cats are wonderful to potty train. Unless they have an ego, arrogance, or are very stubborn, they should be a great fit. They often take less time than most cats.

6. Tovah - The Good Cat

Birthdate and Departure: Tovah was about 5 months old when she came into our lives, verified by the vet as well. I estimated her birthdate to be around April 15, 2011.

In 2015, Tovah and Katana were relocated together to a wonderful home, where I knew they would be very well cared for. Happily, they successfully re-learned potty training, and have been going ever since. (See Katana next.)

How Tovah Arrived: Two weeks after the death of Loea in 2011, there was a beautiful, very sweet Silver Mackerel Tabby with copper eyes roaming around in a bank's parking lot. The employees had noticed she was dropped off there before the 3-day holiday weekend started. They were very alarmed when upon their return they saw this lovely kitty was still there at the bank. She had been surviving on grass and an old salad someone left for her. (Rabbit food is not proper for a cat, I'm sorry!) The bank employees begged for someone to please to take her home because they were afraid that she "would get run over in the parking lot". After bringing her to the vet, she was de-wormed and brought back to health, and we adopted her.

Assessed Traits: Tovah is the epitome of the Good Cat. She is also Confident, Intelligent, at times Stubborn, and is a very healthy and well-adjusted Top Cat.

Life with Tovah: Indeed, Tovah means "good" in Hebrew, and she lived up to her name, putting up with ear drops, de-worming medicine, thorough flea combing, and claw clipping without even knowing me for more than a few days. She loved to play "stringy" just like Loea did.

Some unique features of Tovah are that she was extremely communicative. Having a fairly soft voice, she would use very exaggerated body language, like putting her head upside down when she wanted to get your attention. What was really unusual is that she most especially used her paws as though to do sign language. This was totally spontaneous, and I had never seen a cat do this before or after. There were several signs she would make regularly, one for

interactive playing, in which she would make gestures just as though a human would to wind string. Another sign she did was for when she was hungry, and she would put her paw up to her mouth, gesturing as though to eat food with her hands. She would also frequently put her paw down from her mouth. I was very curious. I knew a sign language interpreter, and asked if any of these signs had actual meaning. I repeated Tovah's gestures, and indeed, each had a distinct meaning in American Sign Language (ASL). The winding motion, although a bit abstract could very well mean "winding" as for string, which was her favorite game. The other two frequent signs were spot-on! Putting her paw to her mouth, was in no uncertain terms the sign for "eat", and the putting her paw down from her mouth was, "good". The interpreter told me, "Aw, she's saying her name!" Tovah would also scratch at a closed door much like a dog if she wanted in a room where the door was closed. I don't think I have ever known such a communicative kitty.

Tovah is a born "Top Cat", but very well-adjusted, caring for and nurturing her fellow felines. She would get into it with Mima, who was not at all well-adjusted, and vied for the position of Top Cat. As time went on, the two would get into very bad fights, and they finally had to be separated.

Potty History: She started potty training and breezed through it, enduring some terrible bouts of diarrhea that she had since she arrived no doubt due to her poor diet. After switching to some better food, she did have a bit less, but still had some blood and much mucus toward the end of her stool. The vet assured us that this was a relatively normal thing, and she checked out okay. Even though she was "loose", Tovah still strained and pushed, apparently feeling like there was more in there to come out. Another issue was that she had not been spayed yet, and had terrible heats that made her so nervous that she couldn't keep anything down. The vet said that she was going to continue to get sicker and for her health's sake, she had to get spayed. That did the trick. Between a premium diet and no more heats, she gained weight, stopped having loose stools with blood, and was far calmer. Tovah was good about going on the potty unless it was dirty and needed flushing, in which case she sometimes would go next to the toilet.

141

When we had to relocate, we moved to a location where a shower door was impossible to be installed, not for lack of trying. (I should have made a bathtub screen!) To complicate matters, the drain plug didn't work, and nobody was able to fix it. Filling the tub with water was simply not an option. During that period of several months, she kept going in the bathtub. Her going "#2" was in various tub areas, and "#1" was directly on the bathtub drain. I don't know what it was that attracted the two cats to this bathtub so much, but they seemed to like going there. It is highly likely that it was because the toilet was an extra-high model, and there was absolutely no room for a step stool in the bathroom, that they felt this was a safer place to go. At least she and Katana were later retrained under more favorable conditions.

Conclusion: Here again, Good and very Intelligent cats without ego, are very successful potty trained.

7. Katana - The Digger

Birthdate and Departure: According to the shelter people and vet records, Katana was born around April 15, 2011, so she was pretty much the same age as Tovah, which is probably why they are so close.

Along with Tovah (see prior story), due to an allergy situation, they were relocated to a wonderful home in 2015, where they are still happily going on the toilet.

How Katana Arrived: After several weeks, I thought Tovah could use a friend. We drove to a local pet super store, and they happened to have cats for adoption. Since it was near the holidays, there was even an "adopt-one-get-one-free" sale going on. I found a pretty, very large Calico semi-longhair, who is the cat in the next story. Katana was the second of the "BOGO". I came to pick up the Calico,

and was initially looking for an older cat who would be harder to adopt out. Instead, they brought me this adorable Patched Tabby/Calico kitten named "Garland". It was a cute name, but she was so small she just had to be "Katana". (Katana means "little", and being gender-based, "little girl", in Hebrew.) Her tail was as thin and small as a pencil, and she had unusually short, soft hair. Her mother, a beautiful, sleek Tortoiseshell was in a cage but not being adopted out yet. I asked were they sure that they didn't want me to take an older cat? They insisted. Katana was very well loved and they wanted her to go to a good home. It turned out she was a bit "special".

Assessed Traits: Katana was a "Digger", who would scratch and scratch ferociously at the litter and the potty seat. She is also a "Not-So-Bright" Cat, who looked at things a little differently, kind of being in her own little world. She appeared to be a Young Cat, but according to the vet records from the shelter, she was the same age as Tovah.

Life with Katana: At first Katana was somewhat of a

terror, getting into things, and going places where she wasn't supposed to. The shelter workers said this cute little kitty was a "social eater" who tended to not eat unless someone was standing there with her, petting her and watching her. Later on, she must have developed  enough confidence to grow out of that phase, because she became a voracious eater with a huge appetite for anything, stealing food from felines and humans alike!

She grew very quickly, and became almost the same size as Tovah if not slightly bigger. Although somewhat mentally challenged in certain areas, she has a sweet charm about her in her blissful innocence. Always very positive and perpetually kitten-like, she can cheer anyone up. She is just so much fun! Katana is rather fearless, being somewhat oblivious to danger. Most of the time she is rather robotic in nature. She didn't quite grasp the concept of a mirror like most cats do, and tried to dig her way through to the other side. She enjoys playing with furry "mousies" and with "stringy", but these were sometimes a bit tame for her taste.

145

Katana is a happy little girl without a care in the world, and she so loves to play roughhousing, physically active games. One of her favorite activities was to go "Swinging". She would get into the center of a bed sheet, and the corners were gathered together like a hammock. Then she would love to be gently swung back and forth from side to side. (If she were human, she would probably be a big fan of amusements park rides.) She also liked to be spun around in a swiveling office chair. Another game was "Bullfight", where I would hold up a towel, say, "Toro, Toro!" and she would charge at it, pass under it, repeat it, and finally I'd toss the towel over her head, and she would plop down on her side. She just loved these physically active games and would play nearly all the time. Everything developed into a game. Even a mundane item like a scratching post had the potential for fun, as she would launch off of her eating shelf, grab onto it, tackling and bunny kicking it. Sometimes she would spin around on it in circles as she hugged it.

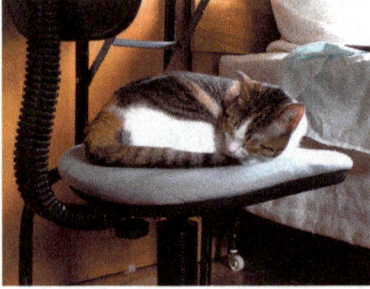

She would sometimes play-fight with the much larger Temima, but eventually got hurt in the process. (See

Mima's intertwined story afterwards.) She stopped eating, and developed a high fever, so we took her to the vet, where they discovered a small scratch on her eye. After antibiotics (which Katana actually loved the pink bubblegum liquid), Katana got back to normal.

Eventually, Katana took a liking to rolls of toilet paper, and discovered that they were kept under the cabinet. (She did do a few relatively smart things, like open cabinet doors to the point where I had to tape them shut.) She would sometimes open the cabinet, grab a toilet paper roll (almost as big as she was) and cart it off into the bedroom for some play time of unrolling and chewing it up.

One of her funniest habits (which she learned from watching Temima) is to drink water with her cupped paw, much like a human would. She would dip her paw in, swipe to cup the water, bring it straight up to her mouth, and lap it up. She would repeat it until either she had her fill or was caught in the act, at which point she would stop and drink like a normal cat. She even did this with food at times.

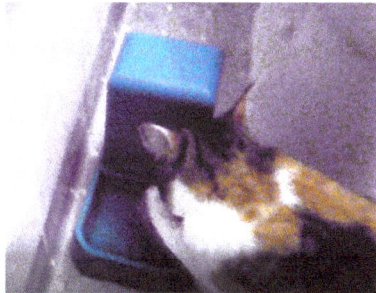

Potty History: Katana trained excellently, and used the potty flawlessly like a robot, but was a Digger. She dug furiously at the litter, the toilet seat, the tank, and the trainer,

often with both paws like a dog. (See Tovah's story earlier, on when we moved to a place with no shower door. She decided to try using the bathtub instead of the toilet, going precisely on the drain without a missed target.) As in Tovah's story, the two are again potty trained in a new location.

Conclusion: The Not-So-Bright Cat is actually *very easy to train* because they don't over-think things, and are more "robotic" in nature. Usually, they are highly motivated by food treat rewards, and it works very well for them. You should have no trouble training this type.

8. Temima - The Top Cat

Birthdate and Departure: Temima was estimated to be around two years old by the shelter workers, and her adoption date was substituted as a birthday, which I think was December 27, 2011.

In 2014, she was relocated to a friend of the family who fostered cats and kittens for a shelter, and always kept a litter box. It turned out that Mima fell in love with her new Pet Parent, the two are inseparable, and this formerly elusive girl actually became a "Close Cat" with her. Mima had finally found her forever home, so it is a happy ending.

How Temima Arrived: "Mima" came to us in late 2011, a very healthy cat. She was a very large, fluffy Calico with a slightly longer coat than a shorthair. (See Katana's story just before for more details, since these two stories are directly intertwined.) I was observing her, and she even demonstrated that she would likely be a good potty candidate. (No Tail-Raising.) I filled out the adoption

149

paperwork, and was to pick her up at the shelter in a few days when I was approved. The huge shelter located in what was probably once a warehouse, was like being in cat heaven! Kitties everywhere roaming around free, eating from big bowls of food, climbing cat walkways, and trees.

I came to pick up the big Calico they called "Moeller", and the shelter workers related how this group of 11 cats were rescued from a rough location where the owner (who was relocated for whatever reason) had been feeding them. They said they had "named this group of rescues all after Catholic Monks". However, "Moeller" just did not seem like a nice name for her. It sounds more like a tooth

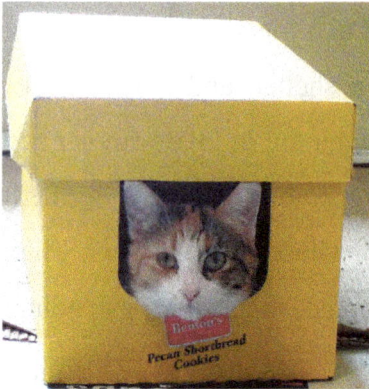

needing to be pulled! I renamed her "Temima", or "Mima" for short, which means "perfect" in Hebrew. I thought that Temima may have possibly been Katana's grandmother.

Assessed Traits: Her most prominent trait was her longing to be Top Cat (although she was more the Unstable Bully type). She was also Arrogant, Confident, slightly Furry-Footed, and in the end had a tendency to be somewhat Spiteful due to being depressed mourning the loss of a loved one.

Life with Temima: Temima proceeded to try to work her way up in cat ranks. Katana didn't care about ranking, but Mima seemed a bit jealous of Tovah, who was the kitty we got her for as a friend in the first place! Mima played extremely rough during her play fights with little Katana who was half her size, and would hurt Katana. On more than one occasion, Mima would get Katana in a backwards bear hug and kick Katana's head, raking at her face with her back claws. She ended up scratching Katana's left eye, and it got an infection.

She would also pick fights with Tovah, which were not always so "playful", and they could get heated. Mima wanted to be Top Cat, but Tovah was there first. Mima would throw her powerful large body against both Katana and Tovah in play fights, and was usually the instigator, which earned her the nickname of "Sumo-Kitty".

Mima did have many endearing traits, such as when scratching on her scratching post, she would always end the session by summersaulting on it. She taught Katana how to drink water with her paw cupped. Her favorite nightly game was to walk around the room carrying a toilet paper tube while calling out the most hideous meowing as though she were about to die. This lasted for several minutes, and then she would curl up and go to sleep. She was very good about doing what she was told. When she is happy, she kind of "skips" as she runs, like a child.

Potty History: Mima actually potty-trained fairly easily, and was quite obedient. I would have never known there was a problem with her. Although at first, she fell in the water a few times, it didn't seem to faze her. She flawlessly went on the toilet, but unbeknownst to me at the time, she apparently just didn't like it. She was healthy and fit, but had had some severe personality issues, which escalated over time. When Tovah refused to back down from being Top Cat, and someone close to her moved out of the household, Mima turned on me! She made her grudges personal. One night, she got up on my bed as I was going to sleep, and sat on my stomach. I was delighted that she was finally giving me some positive attention, when I suddenly realized that I was feeling a warm, damp sensation on my stomach. She wasn't just sitting on me;

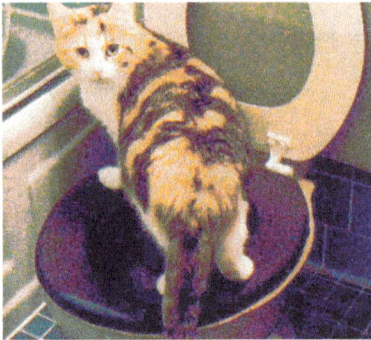

she was squatting there to relieve herself! Granted, I was not as calm as I should have been perhaps. After three different occurrences of this, enough was enough. I think she was grieving for someone who had left the household, and blamed me for their departure.

Conclusion: Mima is a perfect example of the principle that one should be close with their cat to train them. Mima just simply didn't like me! Another factor is that her ego got in the way. Just like an Arrogant Cat, an unstable Top Cat with clashing personality conflicts is usually not well-suited for potty training. Under other circumstances, like being a single cat, I believe that Mima could still be going on the potty without problem.

9. Katerina - The Water Lover

Birthdate: Born on March 31, 2020, Katerina is still slightly less than a year old at the time of this book being published.

She lives happily with me, my husband and "brother" Frankie, who is unrelated by blood, but the two relate to each other like a very close brother and sister.

How Katerina Arrived: I was "cat-less" for almost 5 years, having married a man with mild cat allergies. Then, I discovered the fact that Siberian Forest Cats were potentially hypoallergenic to certain types of allergy sufferers. My husband was happy to learn of this and bought a beautiful 14-week-old girl from a breeder called "Kender Siberians" as a belated birthday present for me in 2020. To our delight, he had only a slight tickle in his nose the first day and was fine after that.

Katerina (our "cover girl") is that special kitty, a Silver and Black Mackerel Tabby. I named her before I even met her, but her name seems to match well, and is befitting our Siberian "princess". After 6 months of age, she grew a beautiful "mane" as you can see on the front cover. (On the back cover she was still just a kitten.)

Assessed Traits: She had several traits that worked for her, and some that worked against her. Mainly, she is quite the Water Lover! She is also a Confident, Disciplined, Furry-Footed, Intelligent, and a Digger. Also, very Stubborn, but when all the lengthy potty training was done, she turned out to be a very good trainee. She is a well-adjusted Top Cat.

Life with Katerina: Katerina is an extremely Disciplined

Cat that knows exactly how she wants her life to be in every way. I had never seen an "OCD" cat before in my life, until I met Katerina! She is Intelligent, a very complex thinker, and enjoys creating new, original games.

As a kitten, she mastered Hide and Seek, but then started inventing her own, more challenging games. One such game was the "Turtle Race" where she would maneuver her head underneath a paper bag on the floor,

and balance the bag so that it was on top of her crouching body. Then with the bag still on top of her like a turtle's shell, she would run as fast as she could, so that all you could see was a bag moving across the floor with little legs running underneath! The game continued as far as she could go without the bag falling or getting knocked off by bumping into furniture.

As she got older, she invented "Charging Tag". She would silently hide underneath the bed, just waiting for an unsuspecting person to come by. When I

would pass by, she would shoot out from under the bed onto her hind legs, jump up and tackle me with her front legs then shoot back under the bed again. If I were not paying attention, I would never even know what hit me, she did it all so fast! It had to be put in frame-by-frame slow motion to be even be able to see her in the video that caught it.

A cute game that she invented by accident, was when she was investigating, and fell into the brand-new small bathroom trash can. At first, she looked quite insulted that we were laughing. Later, she decided that forever more, no small trash cans in her house can ever have bags in them, and she'll physically take the bags out, and play in the empty can for hours.

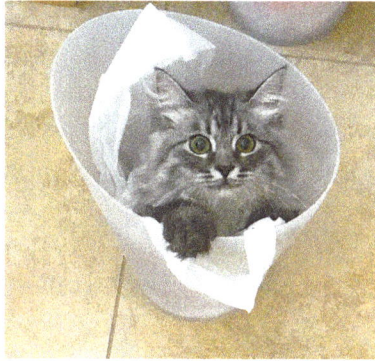

Katerina has created her own routines for everything from feeding methods to her potty schedule. She must have her vitamin supplement at breakfast in the morning. In order to finish it all, our spoiled Siberian princess must lick the remainder bit by bit from off of my fingers held to her mouth. She has a practical reason for this. At a certain angle, it tended to dribble onto her ruff, and she has a hard time washing it due to a short neck and super-long hair. As she was young and teething, Katerina was served a "stew"

of dry food mixed with water and some raw-diet meat, and for a while preferred to let her dry food wait and get soggy for dinner (exactly how she liked it). After she finished her teething stage, she ultimately concluded that no two food types must ever be allowed to touch each other in her bowls. (We use 3 separate bowls, but she is happy.)

Another routine, at least until Frankie came, was that she must play "fetch the springy toy" with my husband every night just before going to sleep. He would flick them out into the room, she would run after them, pick them up in her mouth, jump back on the bed and drop them in front of my husband. They would play this game for perhaps 15 minutes straight until Katerina got tired. She dearly loves her colored spring toys, chasing them around and carrying them in her mouth. That is the top favorite toy of the household, even over the classic furry "mousies".

Katerina enjoys being combed and it puts her to sleep most of the time. She walks proudly with her tail in the air, her fluffy tail bouncing and fur fluffing like a cheerleader's pompoms as she walks. She has perhaps the most expressive face of all of the cats I have ever had. She likes to wash my face, and Frankie's as well. Indeed, Katerina is our spoiled little princess who runs the household. After a while, she saw another kitty come into our back yard and she watched him from afar. He looked just like her! She became somewhat obsessed with him, running to the glass patio door every morning to try to catch a glimpse, or have a staring contest with him. I thought that perhaps she was lonely for another kitty. Then I looked into getting her a companion.

Potty History: Katerina has the distinction of taking the longest time for potty training of any of my cats, at 4 months.

When she was new to our home, she used a litter box in the bathroom for one week, although she refused to go for the first 36 hours. This seems to be a fairly typical behavior for

new cats. Ever since then, she has kept to her own very specific (and highly unusual) potty schedule, regardless of whether it was a litterbox, trainer, or toilet.

When Katerina first came, we used a large roasting pan filled with litter for Part 1 of PHASE 1. She was potty-trained using a simple aluminum Dutch Oven Liner that fit perfectly inside our round toilet bowl under the seat. (See "Simple Trainer" under DIYs on page 171.) Each phase took her an extra-long time because she refused to go for the first 24-36 hours every time there was a change. Quantity vs. Quality- the quantity, (or number of times experienced), was too little so it took her over twice as long to be trained (4 months!) as it would have for a "normal" cat.

When she did go, she liked to dig and throw the litter

everywhere. As the litter got less and less, she still dug. When PHASE 3 started, she liked to dig at the center hole in the water. As PHASE 3 progressed, she liked to play in the toilet water. She was successfully trained, but sometimes had a harder stool and would go on the floor next to the toilet. It wasn't often, so it isn't really a failure in training, she was just having a hard time going, and it was easier than balancing.

True to her Disciplined "OCD-like" nature, Katerina

has a very precise "potty schedule" that she follows. I have never known any cat to do this, except for her. She must go both ways in the morning before breakfast, and then either will go "#1" once at night or she will skip it if it gets too late. If she doesn't go "#2" that morning, she refuses to eat, and will usually wait until night (which is not common) or will more likely just skip a day, holding it until the next morning. There is no compromise, and no in-betweens. Maybe once or twice has she *ever* gone either way during the middle of the day, but that is extremely rare.

To further illustrate her disciplined nature, if she goes potty in the guest bathroom toilet, the treat must be served in the guest bathroom sink. If she went in our master bathroom potty, the treat must be served in a sink there. If it was not done "her way", she actually refused to eat her treat.

Since she is a Water Lover, she didn't care if she slipped off of the modern seat (see front cover) in our master bathroom. She enjoyed falling in and getting wet, and seemed to take the curvy and slippery seat as a fun challenge. (In the picture above, she had just gotten a foot bath after one such event.) Katerina would come in the shower with us if we let her! (She has attempted to on several occasions.) Tired of cleaning up after her water escapades in our bathroom, I finally put my foot down and closed the door so that she could no longer use it. I made her a custom Double Cat Toilet Seat covered with clear non-slip adhesive tape for the guest bathroom toilet.

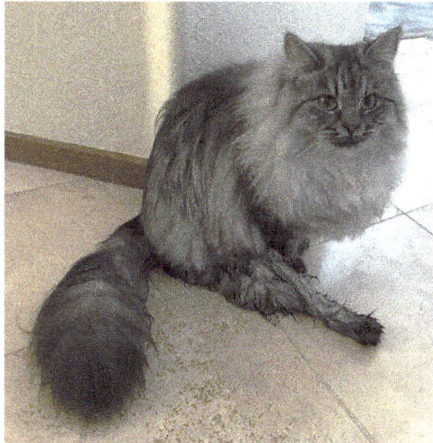

Her "Potty Ritual" is to jump up, go across the seat, get

down, jump up, walk all around, go from one side straight across to the other and back, go down in the bowl, scratch in the water, meowing with the most pitiful tiny meows the entire time. Often, she will get down and leave for quite some time, then return later and do it all again when the urge strikes. When she does finally go, she has her rump all the way down in the bowl only slightly higher than the water itself, as she is perching on the seat.

Early on, being a Furry-Footed Cat, she had a tendency to

slide into the toilet bowl, so I bought a Travel Kiddie Potty Seat. She was fine with it, and it kept her from digging in the water. She was getting too big and outgrowing it though. When her "little brother" Frankie came, during his 2-day "quarantine" in the guest bathroom, she was forced to use our toilet with the Kiddie Seat. Once Frankie got out of his quarantine, and she saw that he used the "baby seat" in the guest bathroom. She then refused to use the toilet there. For a few weeks we had "his and hers" feline bathrooms, and she graciously allowed us to use our own master bathroom toilet. Katerina did help to demonstrate and teach Frankie potty training. Cats do tend to teach each other. (For bad or good.) Katerina has become a healthy and well-adjusted "Top Cat" over Frankie, who blindly obeys her every whim. They clearly adore each other though.

Conclusion: A Disciplined Cat will be easily potty trained, as long as they aren't too Stubborn.

A Furry-Footed Cat needs some sort of help in order to keep from potentially sliding into the water. There are several options available, and I used them all.

One small drawback for a Water Lover, is if you use the Dutch Oven trainer pan method, it sits very deep in the bowl, and get used to that depth. For a while after Graduation, Katerina tended to stand with her hind feet in the water in the toilet bowl, with front feet on the seat and go "#1". This would make a huge mess, as the urine would trail down on her fluffy britches, into the water, and on her feet instead of going out and away from her body in a stream. Fortunately, she usually gave advance notice on her potty use, and I could direct her hind feet up onto the seat before she went. She finally got the idea. Water Lovers are trainable, but may need a little extra attention.

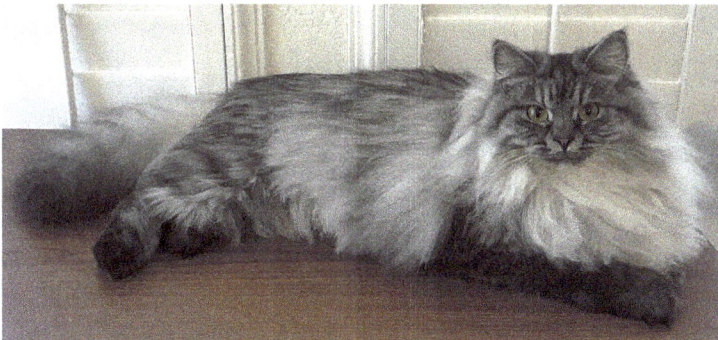

10. Frankie - The Affectionate Cat

Birthdate: Born on July 3, 2020, Frankie is still less than a year old at the time of this book being published. He lives happily with me, my husband, and "sister" Katerina. The two relate to each other like a very close brother and sister.

How Frankie Arrived: Frankie (named for Frank Sinatra), who is 3 months younger than Katerina (see the previous story), was gotten as a companion for her. He is also a purebred Siberian Forest Cat, a Blue and White Mackerel Tabby with a cute "smudge" on his left cheek, and a very long tail for his size. He came to us at a little over 4½ months old in 2020. I saw him in some videos on the Kender Siberians Facebook page, and was struck by his loving demeanor (always purring and kneading) and sweet, soulful eyes. I got the impression that he would be just perfect, and complimentary to Katerina, and indeed, they are "a match made in Heaven".

164

Although they are extreme opposites in many ways, this "odd couple" just seems to click.

Assessed Traits: At time of training, he was still a Young Cat. He is an Affectionate, Obedient, Furry-Footed, Good, and a Fastidious Cat (Except with water). Originally, he was billed mainly as "The Water Hater", but by the time of publishing he had almost totally conquered his fear.

Life with Frankie: Frankie was an intense Water Hater, terrified of any water that wasn't meant to drink. Oddly enough, one of his favorite lounging places is in the bathroom

sink. (Without any water of course.) Katerina basically helped him build his confidence. By watching her (a Water Lover) on the toilet, Frankie learned that the water wasn't going to hurt him. I believe his Travel Kiddie Potty Seat helped immensely as well. He is now so confident that he also tests the water and digs at it slightly, before going potty. (Then again, anything he sees his big "sister" doing, he has to do too.) Frankie is a very Affectionate Cat, who loves to knead and curl up on my lap. He likes to "feline kiss" by gently brushing his cheek against mine. He walks around with his extra-long tail in the air, petting everyone with it as he goes by.

He's a voracious eater, so much so that I had to ration his food so that he wouldn't get intestinal irritation and subsequent diarrhea from gorging. Fortunately, he is relatively polite, and lets Katerina finish most of her food before trying to see if she has any leftovers, as long as I'm within sight.

Frankie is a Good and extremely Obedient Cat, who never does anything he shouldn't. It simply isn't in his nature to do something wrong. If I do my "Ooh Siren" sound when Katerina has done something wrong, he will flee the scene, just to make sure it is known that he was not involved.

He's very docile, and content with Katerina being "Top Cat" to rule the roost. When he first came, he was so timid being in a new environment that he hid under the sofa for 2 days. He was finally coaxed out and kept quarantined in the guest bathroom. I stayed in there much of the time the first couple of days, just spending time with him and bonding. This way he could slowly get used to the sounds and smells before

166

meeting Katerina. Thankfully, after the two first met, they turned out to be inseparable. Katerina and Frankie continue to share their lives with us, (and Katerina shares her toys with Frankie). When she was younger, Katerina had a ritual play time, but that ended when she decided she preferred to just watch Frankie play, usually with the "springy toys". Quite often, Katerina will bring toys to Frankie and drop them down right in front of him, uttering a little squeaky meow. The two constantly talk to each other in little chirpy meows, calling each other to come play, or watch something going on outside. The two love adjusting window blinds, and you can always tell when they have been watching something outside.

Potty History: He has been my best student ever in history, graduating in a mere 27 days without having a single accident or any attempt to go where he shouldn't. In fact, his success was the inspiration that prompted the writing of this book!

He may have scratched at the litter a bit beforehand, but once he "did his business", he would jump right out and go away without even burying it, not wanting to get his paws dirty. Something I had never seen another cat do, is when he's finished and it's time to clean his bottom, this

167

Fastidious boy often tries to bury the smell as he is still sitting there with his leg in the air.

Frankie was a potty training "experiment". I had a theory that since a new cat was not familiar with their surroundings, the raised litter box would not even be an issue. I was right! He was unique in that he was a new cat to the household. Indeed, just as I suspected, he entirely bypassed Part 1 of PHASE 1. The litter trainer pan was put in place immediately, right on the toilet. He took to it without any problem whatsoever, merely needing to see where the litter was. I didn't even have any used litter to add for scent, but he knew what that litter was for! The

trainer also helped cover the water, so he wouldn't see it and be fearful. As time went on and the hole over the water appeared, he started to get nervous. As the hole started to grow, I used the additional aid of the Travel Kiddie Potty Seat. It kept him farther from the water, but he still heard the trickling, and oddly enough wasn't ever bothered by any splashing from below. (And he had some very forceful deposits at times!) It appears that the use of the Kiddie Seat has helped him deal with his fear of the water. Coupled with watching Katerina go on the "big people's" seat without any aid, he now has the courage to go down and sniff at the water and knows that it won't hurt him. Katerina must have taught him that water is okay, and he now can touch the water in the bowl with his paw and not freak out.

His "Potty Ritual" is to whine a lot, jump up on the seat, step straight across many times, get into perfect perching position (sometimes doing a little shuffle) and go. Unlike Katerina, he goes like normal kitties, maybe 4-5 "#1s", and 1-2 "#2s" per day. I strongly believe that his going more frequently also helped him learn quicker due to getting more experience. (Quantity vs. quality.)

Conclusion: Even a Water Hater can be trained to use the potty without problem, as long as they do not fall in. (That could traumatize them and ruin everything!) As with any Good, or Obedient Cat, they train flawlessly and never give any trouble. They are born for potty training!

GRADUATES OF THE
CLASS OF 2020!
FRANKIE & KATERINA
(Left to Right, and Top to Bottom).

Appendix

D.I.Y. Projects for the Handy Cat Lover

There are several fun and useful D.I.Y. projects that one can create to make it even easier for cat toilet training and continued success in it.

🐾 🐾 🐾 🐾

Toilet Trainers

There are many different styles of cat toilet trainers for sale, but these designs work nicely and have had success.

🐾 🐾 🐾 🐾

Simple Trainer

This design does not require one to be especially handy.

🐾 **For Round Toilets:** If you have a round toilet, get a multipack of 12" Aluminum Dutch Oven Liners. They are the perfect size and fit right into a round toilet bowl.

🐾 ***For Elongated Toilets:*** If you have an elongated toilet, a multipack set of approximately 12 x 16" Small Oval Aluminum Roasting Pans should fit nicely. Make sure to measure them prior to purchase.

🐾 ***PHASE 1, Part 2 Trainer:*** It is completely a regular "Raised Litter Box" that fits right into the toilet bowl, filled with clay or preferably flushable litter. (Note: Do not use clumping litter!) Gradually decrease the litter over time.

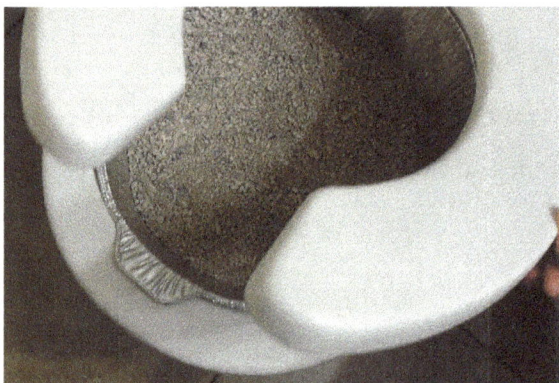

🐾 ***PHASE 2 Trainer:*** Take another Liner or Pan, and set it on an empty cardboard box. Take a nail or screw and poke holes all over the entire bottom. This makes a "Sieve". Put litter in, and gradually reduce it over time.

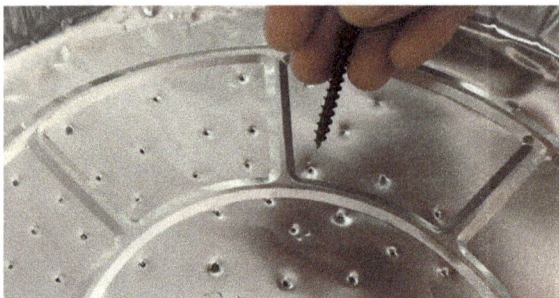

🐾 ***PHASE 3 Trainer:*** Take another Liner or Pan, and set it on an empty cardboard box. Take a box cutter and carefully cut an "X" or a starburst in the center about 3-inches wide. Push the flaps down (toward what would be the toilet bowl water) to create a small hole.

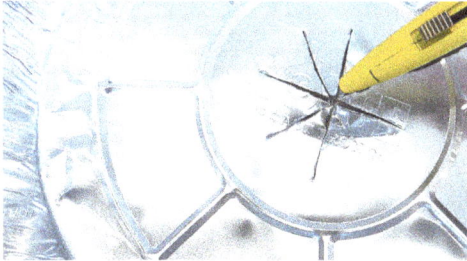

Flip it over, and carefully roll each of the flaps up, and inside of themselves to create a smooth edge all the way around. (This way, if for some reason a cat's paw accidentally went through the hole, there would be no

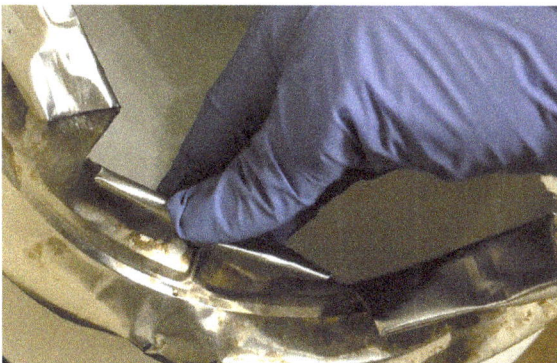

sharp edges to catch on and potentially get cut on.

This pan can be placed over the Sieve pan, then remove the Sieve pan in a day or two so that there is just this one pan with the small middle hole. A tiny bit of litter can be placed in it as before, then reduced over time.

When the Sieve pan is removed, water suddenly appears in the cat's view for the first time. Most cats are rather fascinated by it. It is just small enough of a hole that the water isn't so intimidating to those cats, like the Water Hater.

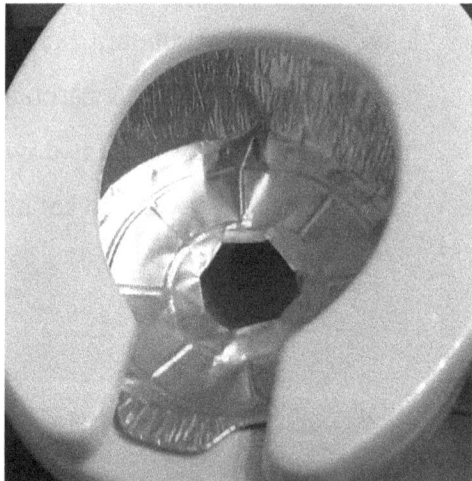

🐾 ***PHASE 3 Trainer Continued:*** There should be no litter at all by now. Take another liner or pan, and do the same as above, only make a star pattern with more than 4 flaps, and make them wider. Roll them up as before. This will continue getting wider each time, every week or two (depending on the cat's progress), until the hole is about 1-inch from the edge of the sides. When the kitty is used to this and has gone at least 7-10 times, it can be removed entirely.

174

🐾 ***PHASE 4 "Graduation Day"!*** Remove the trainer pan entirely, and make sure the cat is supervised constantly. The first time they go will be the hardest, so when they do go, give them an excessive amount of praise and a big treat.

Some cats may hold it for up to 36-hours. Just keep reminding them that they will get a Potty Treat for their efforts. Be sure to let them see you flush it. Most cats enjoy watching their potty get flushed down the toilet. It is quite cute to watch, but they get immensely excited, and know their treat is coming.

The only drawback to the Simple Trainer is that it goes pretty far down into the toilet bowl, and if your water level is too high, it can flood the litter out after PHASE 2. (Not to mentions, it makes it great fun for the Water Lover, or a nightmare for the Water Hater.) There may be a few factors that affect the water level, such as the float device and sometimes even the toilet itself. Fortunately, most cats won't be bothered by a higher water level. Our bowl had a very high water level in comparison to some, so it may not even be an issue. Then again too, if one has a very low water level, no matter what the trainer design, the cat may be tempted to go down inside the bowl to scratch. All the more reason to keep your toilet bowl well-cleaned.

Deluxe Trainer

This design requires a bit more advanced skills than the Simple Trainer, and woodworking tools *are* required.

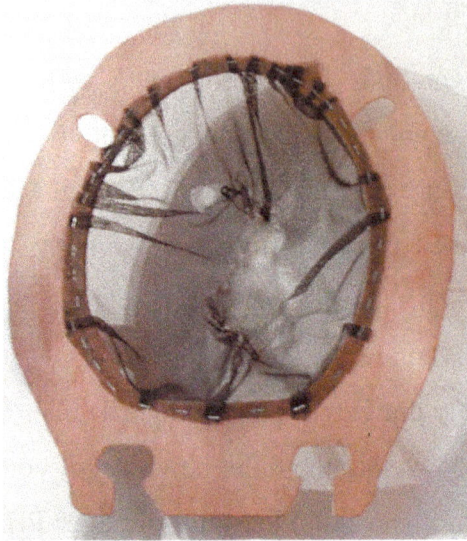

🐾 ***Step 1:*** Take a small square of Lauan board, trace out the toilet bowl on one side, and cut to fit with a band saw or jigsaw.

🐾 ***Step 2:*** Then put it on the toilet bowl. Mark exactly where the hinges fall and cut the area away.

🐾 ***Step 3:*** Mark where the bumpers contact the bowl rim, and drill out that spot. You are left with what becomes a custom insert that fits directly on the toilet bowl rim.

🐾 *Step 4:* Get some flexible plastic window screening. You will be making a small basket, just as though the screen is a basketball net, but without the hole in the middle. Make sure it is a bit loose, ideally bunching it up slightly in the middle. (This is where the litter will go initially.) Be sure that it is not at all taught.

🐾 *Step 5:* Staple the screen into place from the bottom. This is for PHASES 1 and 2.

🐾 *Step 6:* At PHASE 3, you cut a small hole in the center, and it gradually gets larger, then larger.

Ideally, this design makes the cat less comfortable to be sitting in the middle of the litter, so it gradually forces them to gravitate to perching on the seat itself, which is exactly what we want them to do. It was used with great success for at least three cats in a multi-cat household.

This trainer can be kept around for potential future use. After "Graduation", simply remove the old staples and screening, then add new whole screen and staples. It is worth the little extra work to initially put into making it. This trainer stores very nicely and is relatively flat, so it doesn't take up much storage space at all.

Double Cat Toilet Seat

This is designed for coexisting humans and felines, and can be adapted for older cats. It is not at all hard to make, and it is almost surprising that nobody has come out with one commercially. (If anyone does decide to go into business making them, perhaps think of me and I can get a little royalty from it!) Here is a picture of the finished product...

The cat goes on the lower seat and the human can put down the upper human seat when they need to go. This way, if for some reason the upper seat accidentally falls down or was not put up, the cat can still use the toilet.

Optional: Some 2-3-inch anti slip/non-skid safety tape used for ladders and steps. This is an aid for older cats and longhaired cats with furry feet (the "Furry-Footed").

🐾 ***What You'll Need:*** You will need two old-style toilet seats with exposed hinges that have visible screws attaching it to the lid. (On some models, the holes for the seat part are nearly identically positioned as for the lid.)

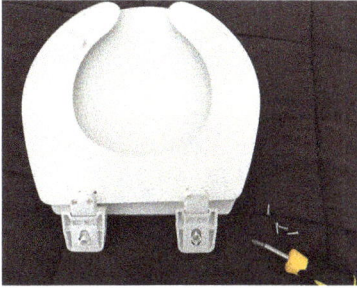

Many fancy modern toilet seats have "hidden" hinges as on the picture to the right above.

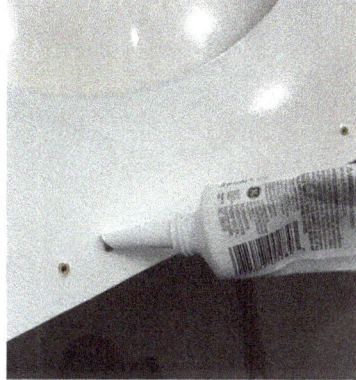

🐾 ***How to Make It****:* Unscrew the lids from both seats, and discard. Unscrew the hinge from the upper seat, so the only part left is the seat itself. If the holes are not in identical places, you will have fill the old holes of the upper (human) seat with a little white silicone caulk (presuming your seat is white).

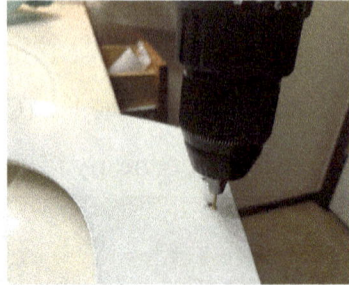

Next, if needed, measure and mark where the lower hinge will be screwed into the upper seat, and make a little pilot hole with a tiny drill bit, but *don't drill in too far*. Now, screw the bottom seat hinge to the upper seat as in the picture below left.

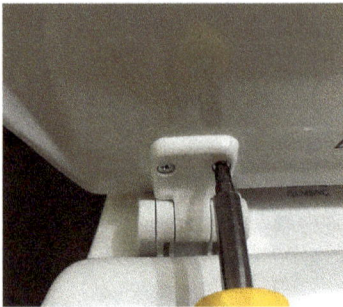

🐾 *Adding the Optional:* Cut strips of the anti-slip tape to cover the surface of the bottom seat.as in the picture above to the right. This isn't *as* easy to clean as the seat itself, but it can be scrubbed well with a sanitary wipe. Since it is designed for bathtubs as well as steps, it is pretty easy to clean. If you only get clear, it will eventually get gray from paw oils. There is plenty to a roll, so replacement is easy!

180

Removable Bathtub Screen Cover

If you don't (or can't) have a shower door, and you are a little handy, you might want to build one of these. It just takes a simple wooden frame with a center support.

A tub cover can be fairly easy to remove, and deters cats from ever wanting to go potty in the bathtub.

🐾 **What You'll Need:** Three 2x3s, staples and a staple gun, wood screws, 8 flat angle braces, and 4 T-braces, a drill, 36" wide (¼, ½, or 1-inch square) hardware cloth (the wire screen-like mesh that is used on rodent cages and rabbit hutches), a wire cutter, and some rubber adhesive cabinet door bumpers. (I wouldn't recommend using poultry netting, due to the potential that a cat could possibly jump on it and get their foot stuck in it.) You can also use some extra-long drywall screws to secure the wood together on the ends and middle.

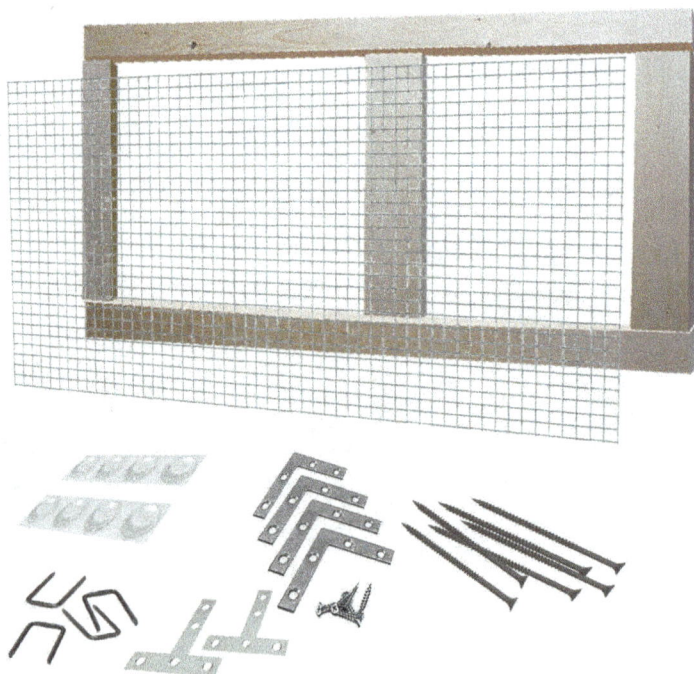

☺ *How to Make It:* Measure out each of the tub's sides. If you don't have the tools to cut the wood, have a hardware store cut it for you. All three of the center pieces should be able to be cut from one 2x3, and the two long ends will need to have the excess cut off. Cut the wood a little bit smaller to leave some slack, because if it is too tight it will scratch the sides or possibly not fit. It usually doesn't hurt to be smaller than the tub, but if it is too big it is not going to work! Cut the two ends and the center support to fit in between the two long side boards.

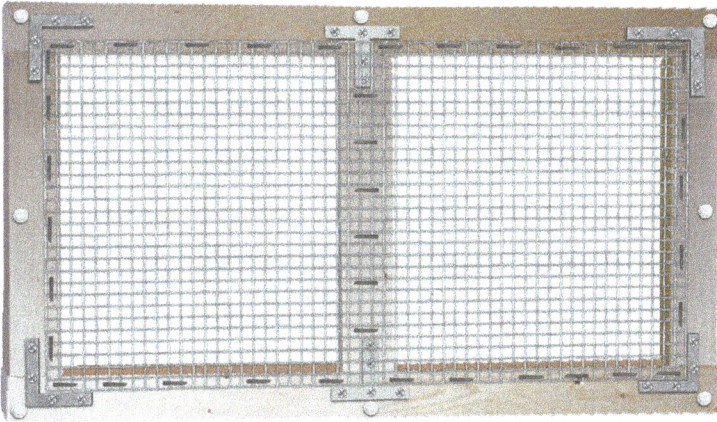

☺ *Step 1:* Lay the pieces on the floor in the way they will be put together. Using small wood screws, affix a Flat Corner Brace on the corners of each of the joints on both sides. Then attach the T-braces on the center piece of wood on both sides, and left and right.

🐾 *Step 2:* Once the pieces of wood are all screwed together, lay the hardware cloth and cut it to fit with wire cutters to the center of the outer wood frame.

🐾 *Step 3:* Now, staple it into place with the staple gun.

🐾 *Step 4:* On the bottom side that will rest on the tub rim (preferably the side with the hardware cloth), stick the cabinet door bumpers all along the frame to keep from scratching the tub rim.

This device was also used once for a very different purpose, to keep a mother cat and her kittens safely contained in the tub! When it was no longer needed, it was the same size as a doorway, and it was converted into a screened door that separated the dining room from the rest of the house at my mother's. It was decorated with lattice.

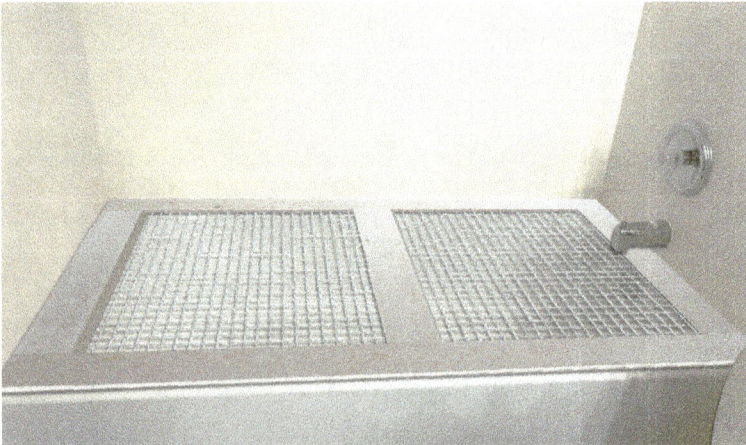

May Your Kitty Graduate!

Congratulations, you now know all there is to know about the potty training business.

May your kitty graduate with flying colors!

🐾 🐾 🐾 🐾

About the Author

Cassie Cluster grew up having many different critters, but always had a special affection for cats. She raised rats for pet shops, endangered turtles for release into the wild, has kept birds, fish, snakes, dogs, rodents, a Dutch bunny, Guinea pigs, small reptiles and amphibians, and even a pet tarantula named Beatrice. Still, none compared to her feline family, and her ability to analyze their various personalities. Cassie shares her practical experiences of toilet training cats over the past 30 years.

www.ingramcontent.com/pod-product-compliance
Lightning Source LLC
Chambersburg PA
CBHW070930030426
42336CB00014BA/2611